JUSTIFIED *by* FAITH

THE APOSTLE PAUL'S PRESENTATION OF THE GOSPEL

JUSTIFIED *by* FAITH

THE APOSTLE PAUL'S PRESENTATION
OF THE GOSPEL

KEN CLAYTON

Justified by Faith: The Apostle Paul's Presentation of the Gospel

ISBN 978-1-955295-40-6

 COURIER PUBLISHING

100 Manly Street
Greenville, South Carolina 29601
CourierPublishing.com

PUBLISHED IN THE UNITED STATES OF AMERICA

Dedication

I dedicate this book to my wife, Joy, a faithful servant of the Lord. We have been co-laborers in the ministry of our Lord Jesus Christ for almost sixty years.

I also thank Joyce and Lonnie Wilkey for encouraging me to write a study of the book of Romans.

ACKNOWLEDGMENTS

As a seminary student, I took an advanced Greek class on Romans. We located each Greek word, studied its tenses, and wrote the possible meanings. Then, we wrote a literal translation of that verse. This thorough study helped me in my preaching ministry over the years. Not only have I preached from Romans many times, but I have also taught Romans in the churches I have pastored.

Using these past experiences, I began to write this study. I have checked my memory with the following three sources:

The Nelson Study Bible NKJV, Earl D Rodmocker, General Editor, Thomas Nelson Publishers, Nashville, 1997.

William Barclay, *The Letter to the Romans,* Westminster Press, Philadelphia, 1957.

Dr. James Strong, John R. Kohlenberger III, James A. Swanson, *The Strongest Strongs' Exhaustive Concordance of the Bible*, Zondervan, 2001.

Table of Contents

FOREWORD

While serving as a student pastor in Tennessee, Ken Clayton was my pastor for sixteen years. During those years, I was under his preaching and teaching consistently. Some of the best of that preaching and teaching was from Romans. I am not surprised that he has infused a new book with his insights into this seminal book of the Bible.

During the years that Ken Clayton was my pastor, my wife and I welcomed our son into the world. The arrival of a baby required us to make many decisions, but one decision was easy. We knew we wanted to name our son Clayton. The life of Ken Clayton (and his wife, Joy) made that a simple decision.

The reason that decision was easy is simple. According to Paul, the gospel exists "for obedience to the faith" (Romans 16:27).

Not only is Dr. Ken Clayton a disciplined and careful student of the Scriptures ...

Not only was he a faithful shepherd to his flock across many decades ...

But he is a living illustration of what Paul was calling for — a child of God obedient to the faith.

I can recommend his newest book without reservations.

— **Richard Ross, PhD**
Senior Professor
Southwestern Baptist Theological Seminary
Fort Worth, Texas

Introduction

Paul wrote his letter to the Romans about AD 58 from Corinth. Paul collected an offering for the Jerusalem church from the churches where he had planted the gospel (1 Corinthians 16:2–4).

Paul wrote that he would soon leave Corinth for Jerusalem: "But now I go unto Jerusalem to minister unto the saints" (Romans 15:25). He had always desired to travel to Rome. Rome was the capital of the largest empire in Paul's day. When Paul was in Ephesus and preparing to go to Achaia and Macedonia again, he wrote: "After I have been there, I must also see Rome" (Acts 19:21). When Paul was arrested in Jerusalem, the Lord appeared to him in a vision and said: "Be of good cheer, Paul; for as you have testified for Me in Jerusalem, you must also bear witness at Rome" (Acts 23:11 NKJV).

Although Paul had not yet visited Rome, he wrote a letter to them. In the opening chapter, he wrote, "For I long to see you" (Romans 1:11). He also wrote: "So, as much as in me is, I am ready to preach the gospel to you that are at Rome also" (Romans 1:15).

Paul realized the journey to Jerusalem meant danger for him. He knew he had enemies there. So in Romans 15:30–31, Paul asked for the prayers of the church in Rome: "Now I beg you, brethren, through the Lord Jesus Christ, and through the love of the Spirit, that you strive together with me in prayers, to God for me that I may be delivered from those in Judea who do not believe" (NKJV).

Paul also shared his desire to go to the church in Rome: "When therefore I have performed this, and have sealed to them this fruit, I will come by you into Spain" (Romans 15:28).

In Romans, Paul does not share as much discussion about practical problems as he does in his other letters. He had never been there and had no first-hand knowledge of their situation. Paul used this letter to explain the Christian gospel, God's plan of salvation, and its impact on their daily living.

There was no error, danger, or false teaching in Rome that Paul knew to address. Instead, he sought to share his understanding of what God had done through the ministry, death, and resurrection of the Lord Jesus Christ.

THE ROMAN ROAD

As a boy growing up, I attended the Baptist church, which was one block from our house. I remember hearing adults talk about the "Roman Road." Later, I understood they were talking about a way to present the gospel. Several key verses were used from Romans to help someone understand what Jesus had done and what they needed to do in response.

This method is still used today and is the basis for most other gospel presentations.

The Bible is clear: "For all have sinned, and come short of the glory of God" (Romans 3:23). This means all people everywhere.

What is the result of sin? "The wages of sin is death" (Romans 6:23). What we earn for a sinful life separated from God is death.

But God has a plan. "But the gift of God is eternal life through Jesus Christ our Lord" (Romans 6:23). Jesus paid our penalty because He died on the cross, taking our sins upon Himself. God's grace is the gift of eternal life when we believe in Jesus Christ as our Lord and Savior.

God demonstrated His love for us when we were still in our sins and did not know Him. "But God commendeth his love toward us, in that, while we were yet sinners, Christ died for us" (Romans 5:8).

But we must accept Jesus as Savior and Lord of our lives. "That if thou shalt confess with thy mouth the Lord Jesus, and shalt believe in thine heart that God hath raised him from the dead, thou shalt be saved. For with the heart man believeth unto righteousness; and with the mouth confession is made unto salvation" (Romans 10:9–10).

God has made us the following promise: "For whosoever shall call upon the name of the Lord shall be saved" (Romans 10:13). Romans 3:21–26 gives another example of Paul's gospel explanation.

God's plan of salvation was to redeem us from sin by the sacrificial and substitutionary death on the cross. On the cross, Jesus declared, "It is finished" (John 19:30). Finished means "paid in full."

The perfect lamb of God was sacrificed in our place so that we might have eternal life. Our part is to receive God's plan by faith. The noun, faith, is found thirty-nine times in Romans, and the verb, believe, is found seventeen times. Faith means to trust and obey, not just know about Jesus. Faith commits to follow Him in obedience.

Romans gives Paul's clearest definition of the gospel message. He explained his missionary zeal when he said of the gospel, "It is the power of God unto salvation to every one that believeth" (Romans 1:16). Paul used the Greek word for salvation that means deliverance. After Paul met Jesus Christ on the Damascus Road and was saved, he was convinced the gospel could rescue or deliver people from their sins. He believed Jesus to be the "author and finisher of our faith" (Hebrews 12:2).

The gospel is offered by God's grace to all people on the condition of repentance of their sins and trusting in Jesus as Lord and Savior (John 3:16; Ephesians 2:8–9, Hebrews 2:3). Through salvation, we are no longer the enemies of God but are His adopted children (John 1:22, Galatians 4:4–5, Ephesians 1:5).

KEYWORDS IN GOD'S PLAN OF SALVATION

Paul used a number of words to explain God's plan of salvation.

First, faith (Romans 1:17, 4:9, 12:6). Faith means to trust and obey Jesus Christ as Lord over our lives. It is more than knowledge about Jesus but involves an allegiance to Jesus and a commitment to follow and obey Him. Faith is how we enter a relationship with Jesus by trusting Him for salvation from sin.

Second, grace (Romans 1:5, 5:2, 12:3). Grace means gift. We can do nothing to earn grace and do not deserve it. It is the unmerited favor of God. This gift of eternal life was made possible by the sacrificial and substitutionary death of Jesus Christ on the cross for our sins.

Third, justification (Romans 4:25, 5:18). The noun justification comes from a Greek verb meaning to acquit. It was a legal term used in the courtroom to pronounce someone innocent of a crime. Paul made it clear in Romans 3:9–20 that all are guilty of sin. The law was given to reveal sin but was not the cure for sin. God planned to send His Son to die for our sins on the cross. When we believe in Jesus as Lord, God declares us righteous. As judge, God declares us righteous by His grace through our faith. Paul wrote, "For by grace are ye saved through faith; and that not of yourselves: it is the gift of God: Not of works, lest any man should boast" (Ephesians 2:8–9).

Fourth, propitiation. This word comes from a Greek word that has three meanings: to appease, be merciful, or make propitiation for someone. The Bible never describes people as trying to appease God. God is described as merciful and providing atonement for the sins of believers through the death of Jesus. Jesus' sacrificial death paid the sin debt we all owed.

Thus, through faith in Jesus, we avoid the wrath of God designed for sin. John declared that God sent His Son to become the propitiation for our sins (1 John 4:10). So propitiation is the satisfaction of God's holy wrath against sin, made possible by Jesus' sacrificial death on the cross.

Fifth, redemption. This Greek word was used to describe the purchase price to buy out of slavery and grant freedom to a slave. Paul used this common term from the slave market to explain how Jesus Christ paid the penalty required by God for our sins. When Jesus gave His life on the cross, He took our place so we did not have to die in our sins and be eternally separated from God. When we accept Jesus by faith, He frees us from the penalty of our sins.

Sixth, righteousness. Righteousness is God's standard of purity.

God is holy, so righteousness is a part of who He is. God is the only One who is always righteous. Israel was righteous when it loved, obeyed, and worshiped only God. When God called Abraham to leave his homeland and go to a new land, Abraham believed the Lord, and God accounted it to him for righteousness (Genesis 15:16). So, the beginnings of Israel are traced to the faith of Abraham, which God reckoned to him as righteousness.

Through our faith in the Lord Jesus Christ, we are accounted as righteous, "even the righteousness of God which is by faith of Jesus Christ unto all and upon all them that believe" (Romans 3:22). "Gentiles, which followed not after righteousness, have attained to righteousness, even the righteousness which is of faith. But Israel ... hath not attained to the law of righteousness ... because they sought it not by faith, but as it were by the works of the law" (Romans 9:30–32). Jesus removes our sins when we come by faith to Him and gives us righteousness.

Seventh, sin. The most common word for sin that Paul used is the Greek word meaning to miss the mark. Paul used several different Greek words to describe our human tendency to rebel and disobey God. God has a plan for our lives. We miss the target when we don't aim at God's plan. Paul explained, "I press toward the mark for the prize of the high calling of God in Christ Jesus" (Philippians 3:14).

Paul notes our rebellious, sinful nature: "For we have before proved both Jews and Gentiles, that they are all under sin" (Romans 3:9). Paul also declared: "For the law of the Spirit of life in Christ Jesus hath made me free from the law of sin and death" (Romans 8:2).

We are forgiven and cleansed from sin by our faith in the Lord Jesus Christ. "And he that doubteth is damned if he eat, because he eateth not of faith: for whatsoever is not of faith is sin" (Romans 14:23).

JUSTIFIED *by* FAITH

THE APOSTLE PAUL'S PRESENTATION
OF THE GOSPEL

CHAPTER 1

OBEDIENCE TO THE FAITH

Paul wrote to a church he had never visited. The church was in the capital city of the world's greatest empire. Paul began by introducing himself to the church.

GREETING

Paul, a servant of Jesus Christ, called to be an apostle, separated unto the gospel of God, (which he had promised afore by his prophets in the holy scriptures (Romans 1:1–2).

Paul called himself a slave of Jesus Christ. This Greek word applied to a person owned and under the absolute command of his master. One of the most frequent titles for Jesus is Lord. Paul thought of himself as not belonging to himself but belonging to Jesus. Jesus had loved him and died on the cross to redeem him and all who believed. Jesus was Paul's Lord and Master.

In the Old Testament, the word slave is often used to describe faithful followers of the Lord. Moses, Joshua, Amos, and Jeremiah were called slaves of the Lord. (Joshua 1:2, 24:9; Amos 3:7; Jeremiah 7:25).

Paul was called to be an apostle. He did not seek the office or honor for himself. Instead, he was called by Jesus to be a witness to "Gentiles, kings, and the children of Israel" (Acts 9:15).

Of Jesus, Paul said, "Concerning his Son Jesus Christ our Lord, which was made of the seed of David according to the flesh; and declared to be the Son of God with power, according to the spirit of holiness, by the resurrection from the dead" (Romans 1:3–4).

Jesus was the promised Messiah, God's Son, and our Lord. Humanly speaking, He was the descendant of David (Matthew 1:1). Jesus was completely human, but at the same time, He was the Son of God. The word declared means designated. Jesus was proven to be the Son of God by the resurrection.

By whom we have received grace and apostleship, for obedience to the faith among all nations, for his name (Romans 1:5).

Paul was given his apostleship when he met Jesus on the Damascus Road. In that encounter, Paul accepted Jesus as Lord, and Jesus gave Paul his orders (Acts 9:1–9). The word "apostle" means "one sent." Jesus made Paul the one sent to the Gentiles. Paul received grace from Jesus, obeyed through faith, and was sent to the nations in the name of Jesus.

Among whom are ye also the called of Jesus Christ: To all that be in Rome, beloved of God, called to be saints: Grace to you and peace from God our Father, and the Lord Jesus Christ (Romans 1:6–7).

Paul addressed his letter to the church in Rome. They were loved and called by God to be separated from the world. The word saint means separated ones. We are not separated for pride, prestige, privilege, or power but for service.

The standard greeting in the Greek world was "grace." The common greeting among the Jews was "peace." Paul used both words in his greeting because they were also key words in the gospel.

PAUL'S PLAN TO VISIT ROME

First, I thank my God through Jesus Christ for you all, that your faith is spoken of throughout the whole world (Romans 1:8).

Paul began with a compliment. He said he thanked God for their faith, which had been a witness to all the Roman world. Paul was encouraged by their faithfulness in this pagan capital city. The church had faults, but Paul focused on their faithfulness. If we try to find fault with people, we will probably find it. But when we encourage believers, their lives can rise to new service levels.

For God is my witness, whom I serve with my spirit in the gospel of his Son, that without ceasing I make mention of you always in my prayers (Romans 1:9).

Paul did not personally know all the people of the church in Rome (Romans 16:1–16), but he prayed for them without ceasing. Our Christian duty is to intercede on behalf of others to the Lord. It is a great privilege to come into the presence of the Lord in prayer. Paul understood that prayer was a large part of his service in the gospel of God's Son.

Making request, if by any means now at length I might have a prosperous journey by the will of God to come unto you (Romans 1:10).

Paul now came to one of the purposes of his letter. He wanted the church to know he had also been praying that it would be God's will for him to go to Rome. Paul knew he needed to pray not only for his ministry but also for the ministry of fellow believers. Jesus felt the need to spend time in prayer with His heavenly Father. "And when He had sent the multitudes away, He went up on the mountain by Himself to pray" (Matthew 14:23 NKJV). Prayer should be a consistent priority in our daily walk with the Lord.

For I long to see you, that I may impart unto you some spiritual gift, to the end ye may be established; that is, that I may be comforted together with you by the mutual faith both of you and me (Romans 1:11–12).

Paul desired to go to Rome to teach and share with the believers some truths of the gospel that would help them discover their spiritual gift or gifts and thus give them a firm foundation in the faith. This statement was barely out of his mouth when the Holy Spirit must have prompted Paul to alter his words. In humility, Paul realized that, as believers, they could encourage one another. The faith of the Christians in Rome could strengthen Paul, and his faith would strengthen them.

None of us know all the Word of God. We must continue to grow and learn more of His Word and the lessons of total obedience to Jesus. Along our journey, we should encourage one another. Paul wrote to the church in Colossae that his desire was "that their hearts may be encouraged, being knit together in love, and attaining to all riches of the full assurance of understanding" (Colossians 2:2 NKJV).

Now I would not have you ignorant, brethren, that oftentimes I purposed to come unto you (but was let hitherto) that I might have some fruit among you also, even as among other Gentiles. I am debtor both to the Greeks, and to the Barbarians; both to the wise, and to the unwise. So, as much as in me is, I am ready to preach the gospel to you that are at Rome also (Romans 1:13–15).

Paul wanted the church in Rome to be aware of his desire to visit them for some time, but other challenges in his ministry prevented that from happening. Paul's heart burned with the fire of the gospel, and he wanted the believers in Rome to mature in their faith. He also desired that more people in Rome come to a saving knowledge of Jesus Christ.

Paul had learned from the Greeks and the barbarians. A barbarian was a person whose speech sounded like *bar-bar* or gibberish instead of the refined Greek language. Paul owed a debt to all people, whether educated or uneducated, rich or poor, common people or those of high estate. Paul knew the gospel was for everyone everywhere, and he was eager to share the gospel in Rome.

LIVING BY FAITH

For I am not ashamed of the gospel of Christ: for it is the power of God unto salvation to every one that believeth; to the Jew first, and also to the Greek (Romans 1:16).

The clarity of Paul's understanding of the gospel of our Lord Jesus Christ is beautifully stated in Romans 1:16–17.

Paul began by saying that he was not ashamed of the gospel. Many must be ashamed of the gospel today. Many hide their faith at work or on social occasions with groups of people. There should be no secret disciples. Especially in these dark days, we must take our stand for Jesus Christ and allow the light of His love to shine through us.

Paul endured much suffering for the sake of the gospel. He had been put in prison in Philippi, beaten in Philippi, ran out of Thessalonica and Berea, and imprisoned in Jerusalem and Rome. Yet, he was proud of the gospel.

One reason Paul was not ashamed of the gospel was that he had experienced the power of God to bring salvation to him and countless others. The salvation of God was for everyone who believed. God had begun His plan of salvation with the Jews but had expanded His plan to include the non-Jewish world (Greeks).

For therein is the righteousness of God revealed from faith to faith: as it is written, The just shall live by faith (Romans 1:17).

In God's plan of salvation, His righteousness is revealed from faith to faith. Faith is at the beginning of the salvation process when we trust Jesus as Lord and Savior. Through faith and by God's grace, a person is saved from the penalty of sin and takes on the righteousness of Christ — a right standing with the Father. As believers live by faith, they gain strength from the Lord to overcome the power of sin.

Perhaps the most powerful and life-changing verse in Romans is Paul's quote from Habakkuk 2:4: "The just shall live by faith." True righteousness before God depends on genuine faith in God. Believers are justified by faith. The word "justify" in the Bible meant to account or reckon a person to be right with God. When we, as sinners, are justified, it does not mean we are good or right. Instead, it means God, because of our faith in His

Son, the Lord Jesus, looks at us as if we were not a sinner. God's love and forgiveness treats us as His children and not as sinners and outcasts from His kingdom.

THE WRATH OF GOD

For the wrath of God is revealed from heaven against all ungodliness and unrighteousness of men, who hold the truth in unrighteousness; because that which may be known of God is manifest in them; for God hath shewed it unto them. For the invisible things of him from the creation of the world are clearly seen, being understood by the things that are made, even his eternal power and Godhead; so that they are without excuse: Because that, when they knew God, they glorified him not as God, neither were thankful; but became vain in their imaginations, and their foolish heart was darkened. Professing themselves to be wise, they became fools, and changed the glory of the uncorruptible God into an image made like to corruptible man, and to birds, and fourfooted beasts, and creeping things (Romans 1:18–23).

The unrepentant suppresses the truth about God (18). When people depart from godliness, they suppress the truth about God. They know God is our loving Creator and deserves our worship and praise (19–20). Sinful people know God's mighty attributes because they observe them in creation. They realize He is powerful, yet they suppress the truth about God (20). They have no excuse because they knew about God but were not thankful and did not glorify Him as God (21). They thought they were wise, but they were foolish (22).

The result is always that people form images to worship. These images may be like birds, creeping things, animals, or people. The wrath of God is being revealed against all people's sins and suppression of the truth (18).

The wrath of God is seen throughout the Bible. God is holy and cannot tolerate sin. God's wrath is His judgment on unrepentant sinners. The consequence of our rebellion against God is His wrath. Yet, because of God's love, He sent His Son to die in our place. God made a way out of judgment when a person trusts Jesus as Lord and Savior.

When someone does not believe in God, they want to spread unbelief to others. God is the Creator who loves us and deserves our worship. God has revealed Himself in creation, in His Word, through witnesses, and finally through Jesus Christ. All people are without excuse when they stand in judgment before God.

GIVING THEM UP

Wherefore God also gave them up to uncleanness through the lusts of their own hearts, to dishonour their own bodies between themselves: who changed the truth of God into a lie, and worshipped and served the creature more than the Creator, who is blessed for ever. Amen (Romans 1:24–25).

Paul came to a sad conclusion. Because a person rejected God, God gave them up or abandoned them and allowed them to continue in their sin.

God gives us free will, and He will not force our obedience. We have a choice. Without choice, there would be no love or goodness. Forced love or good behavior is not real love or morality. God sent His Son into the world to die for our sins, but if we reject Jesus, God gives us over to our sins.

As in the parable of the Prodigal Son, our heavenly Father grieves over our decision to turn away from Him. When a person abandons God, sin becomes easier and easier. People invite disaster into their lives through sin. Soon, they are a slave to sin.

In Greek, the word translated "lusts" meant "reaching out after pleasure." The phrase, the lusts of their hearts, means the passionate desire for ungodly pleasures. A person may set his heart on the pleasures of this world and completely forget the Lord. The "Big Lie" (25) is to reject God but lust for the temporary pleasures of this world.

DISHONORABLE PASSIONS

For this cause God gave them up unto vile affections: for even their women did change the natural use into that which is against nature: And likewise also the men, leaving the natural use of the woman, burned in their lust one toward another; men with men working that which is unseemly, and receiving in themselves that recompence of their error which was meet (Romans 1:26–27).

Again, when people abandon God, He gives them over to their choice of an evil lifestyle. These two verses describe the total lack of morals or decency that is the hallmark of our present society. The Roman world of Paul's day was described by writers of the period as a time of prosperity and luxury. Other than the slaves, no one desired to do physical labor. Tacitus, a Roman writer of this period, said, "It is rich in disasters, gloomy with wars, rent with seditions, savage in its very hours of peace. All was one delirium of hate and terror … . He who had no foe was destroyed by his friend" (Barclay 24).

There was such a lack of belief in God that people became immoral and lusted after others of the same sex. Paul called this shameful and said they would receive the penalty for their error. These verses could have been written today. In some states, same-sex marriage has been legalized.

EVIL PEOPLE AND GOD

And even as they did not like to retain God in their knowledge, God gave them over to a reprobate mind, to do those things which are not convenient; being filled with all unrighteousness, fornication, wickedness, covetousness, maliciousness; full of envy, murder, debate, deceit, malignity; whisperers, backbiters, haters of God, despiteful, proud, boasters, inventors of evil things, disobedient to parents, without understanding, covenantbreakers, without natural affection, implacable, unmerciful: who knowing the judgment of God, that they which commit such things are worthy of death, not only do the same, but have pleasure in them that do them (Romans 1:28–32).

These verses contain an extensive list of sins — one of the longest in Scripture. These verses illustrate what happens when a person totally leaves the Lord out of her life. When a person refuses to recognize God, God gives them over to a debased mind (28). They then fill themselves with all unrighteousness (29). The Lord judges all sin. We cannot rationalize our way out of our sin. This list of sins reveals our rebellious nature:

Unrighteousness. The Greek word here translated unrighteousness literally meant not giving to God or others what is due them. This evil person worships and loves himself instead of worshiping God and loving his neighbor as himself.

Sexual immorality. This term applies to fornication, adultery, and homosexuality.

Wickedness. The Greek word behind this word means the desire to harm. This word is also translated as the title for Satan, the evil one. The wicked person is bad and wants to make everyone else as bad as they are.

Covetousness. The Greek word combines two words that mean to have more. It is aggressively striving to have more, no matter how it is gained or who is hurt.

Maliciousness. This is the common Greek word for badness and describes a person with no good qualities. It denotes a person with no morals or good character traits.

Envy. This word describes a person who wants, to the point of anger, what another person possesses or has accomplished.

Murder. Jesus taught that murder included the violent deeds and also the hardened attitude towards others: "But I say to you that whoever is angry with his brother without a cause shall be in danger of the judgment. And whoever says to his brother, 'Raca!' shall be in danger of the council. But whoever says, 'You fool!' shall be in danger of hell fire" (Matthew 5:22 NKJV).

Strife. The meaning of this word is the contention that results from a jealous desire for the position or prestige of another person.

Deceit. The root meaning of this word is to dilute wine or add metals to gold to defraud someone. This word describes the person who twists the truth to gain an advantage over someone else.

Evil-mindedness. The word means evil-naturedness and describes a person who continually has evil intentions.

Whisperers or backbiters. These words describe a gossip who whispers lies to destroy another person's reputation.

Hater of God. Some think God keeps them from their pleasures and doing what they want. They would like to eliminate God so that they could do as they please or so they can become their own god.

Violent. The Greek word translated as violent in the NKJV means pride so arrogant that it opposes God or the actions of a person to hurt or cause grief to someone just for the cruelty of inflicting pain on others.

Proud. Three times, this word is used in the Bible: James 4:6, 1 Peter 5:5, and Proverbs 3:24. More than simple pride, this word carries the idea of contempt for everyone else.

Boasters. The Greek word means one who wanders about, like the old medicine shows where a traveling man bragged about his medicine that would cure anything and everything. So, the word took on the meaning of bragging excessively to impress others.

Inventors of evil things. This phrase describes the nature of evil that it is always seeking new ways to sin. The Bible does not have a complete list of possible sins. When I was a boy, pedophilia was unheard of. The idea of mutilating children sexually to change their sex was never heard of until recent times. Evil people, without God in their lives, will continue to invent ways to sin and rebel against the Lord, moral behavior, moral values, and even common decency.

Disobedient to parents. Is it surprising that this seemingly insignificant sin should be listed in such a sin list? But it is not insignificant to Almighty God. It is one of the Ten Commandments and a valuable truth in a stable civilization. God created humanity male and female and established the family. Jesus called God Father, and Paul declared, *"But ye have received the Spirit of adoption, whereby we cry, Abba, Father" (Romans 8:15).*

Undiscerning. This word means fool or senseless. This kind of person will not use the mind given by the Lord in a wise way.

Untrustworthy. This word means breakers of agreements. There was a time in America when a person's handshake or word was as good as a legal contract. However, a new scam or scheme to swindle people of their money happens almost daily.

Unloving. The word "love" in verse 31 means "family love." Family love was dying among the pagans then and is disappearing quickly in modern society. Baby girls or deformed babies are often abandoned in China and other societies. Millions of babies have been aborted in the United States. Child sex trafficking is a significant business on our southern border and in the United States.

Unforgiving and unmerciful. A lack of forgiveness and mercy characterized Roman society. Life meant nothing. People enjoyed seeing the gladiators kill each other. There were over six hundred murders in Chicago in 2022. Violent crime is at an all-time high in most major cities in the United States. People, separated from the Lord, only care about themselves.

Paul concluded that people without the Lord practice these things and applaud and encourage others to do the same (Romans 1:32).

CHAPTER 2

THE RIGHTEOUS JUDGMENT OF GOD

After exposing the depth of human depravity in chapter 1, Paul declared that God judges all sin. Our rebellious hearts deserve God's punishment. Paul will explain in chapter 2 that God's judgment is righteous and impartial.

JUDGING

Therefore thou art inexcusable, O man, whosoever thou art that judgest: for wherein thou judgest another, thou condemnest thyself; for thou that judgest doest the same things (Romans 2:1).

Paul began with "therefore." Like a good lawyer, Paul had laid out his case that all people had sinned. Now, Paul shares the results of that truth. Since all people are sinners, they have no excuse. Those who judge others are inexcusable. We will be judged not by how we measure up to other people but by how we measure up to God's standards. Judgment will be based on God's truth (1–5), our works (6–11), and God's law (12–16).

But we are sure that the judgment of God is according to truth against them which commit such things (Romans 2:2).

God's judgment is always true and righteous. Jesus said He was the way, truth, and life and that no one could come to the Father but by Him (John 14:6). The word truth in Romans 1:18 referred to the evidence of the truth about God revealed in creation. In Romans 2:2, truth refers to God's judgment of sinful humanity.

And thinkest thou this, O man, that judgest them which do such things, and doest the same, that thou shalt escape the judgment of God? (Romans 2:3).

Paul is primarily writing about the Jews but also about anyone who judges others while involved in sin in their own lives. The Jews believed God would judge the pagans, but they felt He would not condemn them even though they sinned because they were the chosen people. But being a Jew would not save them from God's judgment.

Or despisest thou the riches of his goodness and forbearance and longsuffering; not knowing that the goodness of God leadeth thee to repentance? (Romans 2:4).

Paul accused the Jews of living to please themselves and depending on God's mercy to forgive them no matter what they did. They despised God's goodness, forbearance, and longsuffering. The word goodness means kindness. It is derived from a Greek word for good, meaning a person is essentially kind. Forbearance meant truce and referred to a temporary cease-fire from hostilities. A person must seize the opportunity for peace while it is available.

God was giving the Jews a chance to repent. It was not the freedom to continue in sin but an opportunity to repent and change their behavior. The word longsuffering is a word in Greek that means patience with people. It was used by a person who had the power to avenge a wrong but, in patient mercy, did not. Just because the Jews had not been immediately punished did not mean judgment was not coming.

But after thy hardness and impenitent heart treasurest up unto thyself wrath against the day of wrath and revelation of the righteous judgment of God; who will render to every man according to his deeds (Romans 2:5–6).

God's mercy is not designed to make us think we can sin without consequences. Our sin should break our hearts. Yet many today darken their hearts and are unrepentant. As a result, instead of storing earthly treasures, they store wrath in the judgment of the Lord. In verse 6, Paul quotes Psalm 62:12, "Also to You, O Lord, belongs mercy; for You render to each one according to his work" (NKJV).

To them who by patient continuance in well doing seek for glory and honour and immortality, eternal life (Romans 2:7).

At first glance, we may assume we can gain eternal life by doing good. But Paul teaches that we are justified by faith (Romans 3:22). The subject of verse 7 is judgment, not justification. Once a person is saved, they should do good works for the Lord to show gratitude for salvation. Faith works. James declared, "Thus also faith by itself, if it does not have works, is dead" (James 2:17 NKJV).

Eternal life is a gift received by faith (John 3:16). The final goal is eternal life in heaven for those who believe, and, in the judgment, those who have done good will be rewarded (Romans 5:1; Galatians 6:8; 1 Timothy 6:17–19; 1 Peter 1:7).

But to those who are self-seeking and do not obey the truth, but obey unrighteousness — indignation and wrath, tribulation and anguish, on every soul of man who does evil, of the Jew first and also of the Greek (Romans 2:8–9).

We face many decisions daily. Many of those decisions involve whether to act godly in a situation. God's judgment is based on our claim to be Christians and how we demonstrate that claim by our decisions and behavior. To those who choose to seek only things that gratify themselves or decisions that do not obey the gospel of our Lord Jesus Christ, their actions will result in indignation, wrath, tribulation, and anguish. This is the judgment of everyone who does evil. It doesn't matter if we are a Jew or a Gentile.

But glory, honor, and peace to everyone who works what is good, to the Jew first and also the Greek (Romans 2:10).

Believers who do good works will be rewarded with glory, honor, and peace. The results are the same whether we are a Jew or a Greek. We cannot separate faith and works. If we have faith, we will work for the praises and glory of our Lord Jesus Christ. Remember, faith works.

For there is no respect of persons with God (Romans 2:11).

God does not play favorites. The Jews believed they held a special place of privilege with God. God had called them to a particular place of service. They were to be His witnesses to the world. Believers have also been called to a special place of service in the Great Commission. Jesus gave us that commission in Matthew. Our task is to serve the Lord and obey His commission to "go … make disciples of all the nations, baptizing them … teaching them to observe all things that I have commanded you" (Matthew 28:19–20 NKJV).

For as many as have sinned without law shall also perish without law: and as many as have sinned in the law shall be judged by the law (Romans 2:12).

God's salvation is available to all people, no matter their nationality. Likewise, we have all sinned no matter where we are from. We all will be judged by God's standards. In the Garden of Eden, Adam and Eve were allowed to eat fruit from every tree except one. They both disobeyed God and ate the forbidden fruit. Adam and Eve were given free choice, which included the choice to disobey God.

The basis of all sin is putting our choices ahead of God's. Sin is selfishness and disobeying God's will and plan for our lives. That is true whether a person is a Jew or a Gentile. Unrepentant sin and an unwillingness to follow Jesus result in God's judgment.

For not the hearers of the law are just before God, but the doers of the law shall be justified (Romans 2:13).

Paul returns to the theme of this chapter: practice what we preach (Romans 2:1–3, 6–7, 9–10, 13–14). Just hearing the truth of God's Word does not make us right with God. We are justified or made right with God when we obey His Word.

(For when the Gentiles, which have not the law, do by nature the things contained in the law, these, having not the law, are a law unto themselves: which shew the work of the law written in their hearts, their conscience also bearing witness, and their thoughts the mean while accusing or else excusing one another;) in the day when God shall judge the secrets of men by Jesus Christ according to my gospel (Romans 2:14–16).

Paul mentions those without the written law but who, by instinct, common sense, or nature, obey the things in the law. Since all people are created in the image of God, they possess an intuitive knowledge of right and wrong. That law comes from their hearts or their conscience. One day, God will judge all people, even their hidden sins, by Jesus Christ.

All are under God's judgment — the Jews with the written law and others with the conscience of what is right and wrong. God will judge a person by what he has had an opportunity to know and what he has done with that knowledge.

GUILT

Behold, thou art called a Jew, and restest in the law, and makest thy boast of God, and knowest his will, and approvest the things that are more excellent, being instructed out of the law (Romans 2:17–18).

The Jews felt certain they had a privileged position with God and had His special favor just because they had descended from Abraham and were circumcised. After all, God had revealed Himself to them, and they had the law (17). The Jews knew the will of God, having been instructed by the law (18).

And art confident that thou thyself art a guide of the blind, a light of them which are in darkness, an instructor of the foolish, a teacher of babes, which hast the form of knowledge and of the truth in the law (Romans 2:19–20).

Because of their supposed unique position, the Jews felt they were superior to other people. In their arrogance and pride, they believed themselves to be the guides, light, instructors, and teachers. They held themselves in high esteem. Jewishness is not a matter of race or circumcision. Instead, it involves lifestyle, conduct, and obedience to the Lord.

Thou therefore which teachest another, teachest thou not thyself? Thou that preachest a man should not steal, dost thou steal? Thou that sayest a man should not commit adultery, dost thou commit adultery? Thou that abhorrest idols, dost thou commit sacrilege? Thou that makest thy boast of the law, through breaking the law dishonourest thou God? For the name of God is blasphemed among the Gentiles through you, as it is written (Romans 2:21–24).

With the word "therefore," Paul concludes his point that the Jews are just as guilty of sin as the Gentiles. The Jews taught others but did not obey the precepts they taught. They preached not to steal but stole. They said don't commit adultery, but committed it. They abhorred idols but were being sacrilegious, robbing God of praise and worship. They boasted about knowing the law but broke the law and dishonored God. These Jews thought they were guides and lights, but they broke the laws God had given them. This resulted in the Gentiles blaspheming God (Isaiah 52:5).

Circumcision

For circumcision verily profiteth, if thou keep the law: but if thou be a breaker of the law, thy circumcision is made uncircumcision (Romans 2:25).

Circumcision becomes a useless religious ritual when divorced from a godly lifestyle. A person must commit and obey the Lord for this religious sign to have any value. Being baptized has no value if a person's heart has not been converted by the power of the Holy Spirit, followed by a response of faith in the Lord Jesus Christ. We are saved by grace through faith. We are not saved by church membership, baptism, or other religious rituals.

Therefore if the uncircumcision keep the righteousness of the law, shall not his uncircumcision be counted for circumcision? (Romans 2:26).

If a Gentile kept the law, whether he was circumcised would not matter. God judges a person by their heart, not by external things.

For the Lord does not see as man sees; for man looks at the outward appearance, but the Lord looks at the heart (1 Samuel 16:7b NKJV).

And shall not uncircumcision which is by nature, if it fulfil the law, judge thee, who by the letter and circumcision dost transgress the law? (Romans 2:27).

Like a good lawyer, Paul drives home his point that it is not the outward trapping of religion but genuine obedience that God requires. Now the tables are turned. Paul declared that it would not be the Jews who should be judging the Gentiles. Instead, Gentiles who kept the law would judge the Jews who broke the law. There would be no escape from judgment for these self-righteous Jews.

In Matthew 23, Jesus pronounces a long series of woes against hypocritical Jews. For example, He says, "Woe to you, scribes and Pharisees, hypocrites! For you are like whitewashed tombs which indeed appear beautiful outwardly, but inside are full of dead men's bones and all uncleanness" (Matthew 23:27 NKJV).

For he is not a Jew, which is one outwardly; neither is that circumcision, which is outward in the flesh: But he is a Jew, which is one inwardly; and circumcision is that of the heart, in the spirit, and not in the letter; whose praise is not of men, but of God (Romans 2:28–29).

The outward sign of circumcision was of no value without faithful obedience to the Lord. Our outward behavior must reflect our inward commitment to the Lord. This truth is clearly stated in the Old Testament: "Therefore, circumcise the foreskin of your heart, and be stiff-necked no longer" (Deuteronomy 10:16 NKJV).

Paul described a change of heart that results from the work of the Holy Spirit, not just an external show of following the law. Following all the rituals, sacrifices, and holy days is not the goal. Having a right relationship with God based on His grace and our faith is. As Jesus told Nicodemus, a religious Jew, "You must be born again" (John 3:7 NKJV).

Paul contrasted the two ways of approaching God. The Jewish way was to make themselves righteous by strictly obeying the law. They did not go the way of faith but of the law (31). The Gentiles attained righteousness by faith (30).

In the Old Testament, there were several references to a stone. Genesis 49:24 describes God as the Shepherd and Stone of Israel. Isaiah 28:10 states that God will lay a foundation stone in Zion, a precious cornerstone. In Daniel 2:34–35, 44–45, Daniel prophesied of a stone that would crush worldly empires. Psalm 118:22 tells of a stone the builders rejected and how it would become the chief cornerstone. Jesus quotes Psalm 118:22 and applies it to Himself (Matthew 21:42). Christians in the early church realized that these references described Jesus.

Paul quoted Isaiah 8:14 and 28:16. We can also see the idea of the stone in Acts 4:11, Ephesians 2:20, and 1 Peter 2:4–6. God sent Jesus into the world to be the Savior and Lord over all. When someone trusts Jesus as Lord and Savior, they experience Him as a stone of salvation. But if a person chooses to rebel and reject Jesus, the stone becomes one of condemnation. If we respond to Jesus in faith, we are saved. But if we reject Jesus, we will be judged unfaithful and then condemned.

CHAPTER 3

ALL HAVE SINNED

Paul continued his presentation of the gospel by further explanation of the position of the Jews. He adopts the method of debating an imaginary person representing the traditional Jewish position. Paul had already pointed out there was no difference between the Jew and the Gentile regarding sin, so did that mean they were in the same position?

GOD'S JUDGMENT DEFENDED

What advantage then hath the Jew? or what profit is there of circumcision? (Romans 3:1).

The imaginary debater then asks Paul what advantage the Jew has. Doesn't circumcision mean anything? Do the Jews have no advantage at all?

Much every way: chiefly, because that unto them were committed the oracles of God (Romans 3:2).

The Jews' advantage was that they had received the oracles of God. The word oracles was used for a special message from God, probably here referring to the call of Abraham and the giving of the Ten Commandments to Moses. God entrusted the Jews with commandments, not privileges. The Jews were given special responsibilities, not special privileges. The choice of God to follow Him in obedience carried a special duty and faithfulness. Since the Jews were chosen to obey God and tell the world about the Lord, their position was obedience, not privilege.

For what if some did not believe? Shall their unbelief make the faith of

God without effect? (Romans 3:3).

Some were not faithful to the Lord and did not believe, yet God was faithful to what He had promised. There was always a faithful remnant. God was justified in condemning the unfaithful. Some Jews, like the disciples, believed in Jesus, but the majority rejected Jesus. The task of evangelizing the world was given to the church. Instead of Jews witnessing to the Gentiles, the Gentiles are witnessing to the Jews.

On Mount Carmel, Elijah challenged the prophets and priests of Baal to have their god send fire on their altar. Baal, of course, did not send fire, but the true God sent fire on the altar Elijah had erected. This was a great victory. But when Jezebel threatened Elijah, he fled. He thought he was the only faithful one left. Later, the Lord revealed to Elijah that seven thousand others had not worshiped Baal. The unfaithfulness of some did not stop the plan of God.

God forbid: yea, let God be true, but every man a liar; as it is written, That thou mightest be justified in thy sayings, and mightest overcome when thou art judged (Romans 3:4).

God is the truth. Jesus said, "I am the way, the truth, and the life" (John 14:6 NKJV). God is always justified in His judgments. His promises were fulfilled in the faithful remnant and the believers in the Lord Jesus.

But if our unrighteousness commend the righteousness of God, what shall we say? Is God unrighteous who taketh vengeance? (I speak as a man) God forbid: for then how shall God judge the world? (Romans 3:5–6).

The imaginary debater then asks, "Why shouldn't we be justified because our unrighteousness allows God to demonstrate His righteousness?" This is a foolish human point of view. Although many may think that way, this was an absurd question. The suggestion that God is unjust in punishing sinners is ridiculous. Paul explained that God would not be just if He did not punish unrighteousness. The flaw in the debater's logic is apparent because God's justice demands He judge unrighteousness.

For if the truth of God hath more abounded through my lie unto his glory; why yet am I also judged as a sinner? (Romans 3:7).

This question is basically the same question found in verse 5. This time, the sinner objects to being called a sinner because his sin increases the truth of God.

And not rather, (as we be slanderously reported, and as some affirm that we say,) Let us do evil, that good may come? whose damnation is just (Romans 3:8).

The idea is that the more evil we do, the more good God does. So, people should not be judged for doing evil because God will do more good. This argument is senseless. Although Paul had been falsely accused of saying this, he does not try to argue against it. He knows a just God will condemn people like that.

The root of all sin is disobedience to God. In the Garden of Eden, Adam and Eve disobeyed God and ate the forbidden fruit. Because of their disobedience, the first judgment of God came. They were forced to leave the Garden, and Adam would have to work diligently to grow food. Additionally, Eve would have pain in childbirth. Sin is disobeying the will and word of God for our lives.

The correct response to sin is not to justify it, blame others, or even blame God. The correct response is to humbly repent, confess our sins, and seek God's forgiveness.

UNIVERSAL SIN

What then? are we better than they? No, in no wise: for we have before proved both Jews and Gentiles, that they are all under sin (Romans 3:9).

The Jewish debater asks if that means the Jews have an advantage over the Gentiles. Paul's answer is no, since all people have sinned. In Greek, the phrase "under sin" means "in the power of, or under the authority of." So, a person without Jesus is under the command of or under the authority of sin.

As it is written, There is none righteous, no, not one: There is none that understandeth, there is none that seeketh after God. They are all gone out of the way, they are together become unprofitable; there is none that doeth good, no, not one. Their throat is an open sepulchre; with their tongues they have used deceit; the poison of asps is under their lips: Whose mouth is full of cursing and bitterness: Their feet are swift to shed blood: Destruction and misery are in their ways: And the way of peace have they not known:There i s no fear of God before their eyes (Romans 3:10–18).

To prove his point that all have sinned, Paul strings together several Old Testament passages as a Jewish rabbi would do. He quoted from Psalm 14:1–3, Psalm 5:9, Psalm 140:3, Psalm 10:7, Isaiah 59:7–8, and Psalm 36:1.

Verse 12 contains an interesting word that translates "unprofitable." It means "to render useless." People without Jesus are useless. These verses show that character, conduct, and life are eternally useless without Jesus Christ. Paul realized people without Jesus had no hope. He believed in the depravity of human nature, but he also believed in the redeeming power of Jesus Christ. We all have sinned, but Jesus is a great Savior. Paul knew all had sinned, but all had the opportunity to believe in Jesus and be saved. What Jesus had done for Paul, He could do for anyone.

Now we know that what things soever the law saith, it saith to them who are under the law: that every mouth may be stopped, and all the world may become guilty before God. Therefore by the deeds of the law there shall no flesh be justified in his sight: for by the law is the knowledge of sin (Romans 3:19–20).

The phrase "whatever the law says" (19) refers to the questions from the Old Testament in verses 10–18. The verses indicate that all the world is guilty before God (19).

The work of the law is to bring about the knowledge of sin. No one is made righteous by the law because the law does not justify sinners. Instead, it exposes sin. The way to God is not through the law but by grace. Nor is it by way of works but by faith.

God's Righteousness Through Faith

But now the righteousness of God without the law is manifested, being witnessed by the law and the prophets; even the righteousness of God which is by faith of Jesus Christ unto all and upon all them that believe: for there is no difference (Romans 3:21–22).

The real question is how a person enters a right relationship with God. How can a person have peace and escape the wrath of God? The Jews believed the path to God lay in keeping the law. But it is not possible for humans to keep the law perfectly. Since people are imperfect, how can they perfectly keep the law?

Paul says God pronounces sinners righteous apart from the law. Our sin puts us in a wrong relationship with God. The Old Testament, that is the Law and the Prophets, witnessed this truth. God accounts people as righteous through their faith in Jesus Christ "to all and on all who believe" (22). Faith in Jesus is accounted by God as righteousness.

For all have sinned, and come short of the glory of God; being justified freely by his grace through the redemption that is in Christ Jesus (Romans 3:23–24).

God revealed in His Word how people should live, but no one can live up to God's standards. All of us have sinned and do not measure up to His glory. We cannot save ourselves because we cannot meet God's standards. Our only hope of salvation is faith in Jesus Christ.

Those who believe are justified. By God's grace, those who believe are made righteous. Jesus died on the cross to pay the price to redeem or ransom sinners. Because of the sacrificial death of Jesus on the cross, He can offer His righteousness to those who believe. God took the initiative to bring us into a proper relationship with Him.

By Christ's Blood, Through Faith

Whom God hath set forth to be a propitiation through faith in his blood, to declare his righteousness for the remission of sins that are past, through

the forbearance of God; to declare, I say, at this time his righteousness:
that he might be just, and the justifier of him which believeth in Jesus
(Romans 3:25–26).

In this section, Paul writes a long sentence that stretches from verse 21 to verse 26. In the first part of this sentence, he explains that God grants His righteousness to all who believe in Jesus (21–22). Since all have sinned, the grace provided by Jesus on the cross justifies the faithful (23–24).

As Paul continues this long sentence, he uses an idea from the sacrificial system. Jesus' death on the cross was the propitiation for our sins. The book of Leviticus describes the events on the Day of Atonement (16:15–22). A sacrifice was made for the nation, and the blood was sprinkled in the Tabernacle. The High Priest sprinkled blood on a goat and placed his hand on the goat's head — symbolically placing the sin of the people on the goat. The goat was then driven into the wilderness. Hence, the name scapegoat. All the people's iniquity, transgressions, and sin were placed on the goat, and the goat took the sin away from the people.

Jesus bore our sins on the cross. He who knew no sin became sin for us (2 Corinthians 5:21). Jesus' death fulfilled the Day of Atonement. He was the perfect sacrifice to atone for all sin. Because of Jesus' shed blood, God passed over our sins to reveal His righteousness. God is just and justifies the person who has faith in Jesus. The way to a right relationship with God is not to win God's favor by our works but to humbly repent and accept the love and grace of God offered to us in Jesus Christ.

THE LAW OF FAITH

Where is boasting then? It is excluded. By what law? of works? Nay: but
by the law of faith. Therefore we conclude that a man is justified by faith
without the deeds of the law. Is he the God of the Jews only? is he not also
of the Gentiles? Yes, of the Gentiles also: Seeing it is one God, which shall
justify the circumcision by faith, and uncircumcision through faith. Do we

then make void the law through faith? God forbid: yea, we establish the law (Romans 3:27–31).

Since the way to God is by His grace through faith, all boasting of human effort is in vain. No one can stand before God and boast of their good deeds. The Jews associated the law, God's standard, with works. But God's standard is not met by human works but by the law of faith. When the people asked Jesus, "What shall we do, that we may work the works of God?" Jesus answered, "This is the work of God, that you believe in Him whom He sent" (John 6:28-29 NKJV). The law could only condemn them, but Jesus could save them.

A person is justified or declared righteous apart from doing what the law requires. Salvation is through faith alone. We cannot earn our salvation nor do we deserve salvation. Jesus alone saves, and it is His gift to all who believe.

The Jews had the verse from Deuteronomy 6:4 in their phylacteries and sewn into the hem of their robes: "Hear, O Israel, the Lord our God is One God" (NKJV). There is one God for the Jews and Gentiles. The way to God is the same for all people. It is not by works, but faith. Faith is not the end of the law, but the law can only be fulfilled by a faith relationship with the Lord.

CHAPTER 4

ABRAHAM JUSTIFIED BY FAITH

Chapter 4 is vital in Paul's argument to establish that justification is by God's grace through faith alone. No person would be a greater example to the Jews than Abraham. He was the founding father of the nation and of their religion.

What shall we say then that Abraham our father, as pertaining to the flesh, hath found? For if Abraham were justified by works, he hath whereof to glory; but not before God (Romans 4:1–2).

Abraham, the Jew's example in his flesh, could not earn God's righteousness by works. The phrase according to flesh means according to his labor. Paul was asking if God justified Abraham according to his works. If so, he could boast about his achievements. But God reckoned Abraham's faith as righteousness.

For what saith the scripture? Abraham believed God, and it was counted unto him for righteousness (Romans 4:3).

Paul debated that it is not works but faith that justifies a person before God. This must have seemed like a new doctrine to the works-oriented legalistic Jews. But Paul explained that this was exactly how Abraham was justified. Paul quotes Genesis 15:6 to prove that Abraham was justified by believing God. God made a promise to Abraham, and Abraham believed God. God pronounced Abraham righteous, not because he obeyed some laws or did some works but because he believed God.

Now to him that worketh is the reward not reckoned of grace, but of debt (Romans 4:4).

When a person works to gain righteousness, it leaves out God's grace and keeps the person indebted to God.

Paul was a wise teacher. Some teachers theorize and talk about possibilities or impossibilities. However, a wise teacher uses concrete or everyday experiences to aid their students' understanding. Paul used Abraham as an example of what faith meant because he was a person they all respected.

God called Abraham to leave his home and all he knew to go to a new place that God would show him. Abraham believed and obeyed God. "By faith Abraham obeyed when he was called to go out to the place which he would receive as an inheritance. And he went out, not knowing where he was going" (Hebrews 11:8 NKJV).

The New Testament makes it clear that no person can ever earn or deserve God's grace. All we can do is believe in God and base our lives on the faith that God's Word is true.

THE FAITH OF DAVID

But to him that worketh not, but believeth on him that justifieth the ungodly, his faith is counted for righteousness. Even as David also describeth the blessedness of the man, unto whom God imputeth righteousness without works (Romans 4:5–6).

Paul gave another powerful example of faith by mentioning the most beloved ancestor of the Jewish people, David. David had come to God by faith alone and had not depended on his works. God counted this to him as righteousness. The phrase, justifies the ungodly, probably horrified the Jews. Paul claimed that God accounts sinners who believe in Him as righteous. Righteousness does not come through the law or from following Jewish rituals or tradition.

Blessed are they whose iniquities are forgiven, and whose sins are covered. Blessed is the man to whom the Lord will not impute sin (Romans 4:7–8).

David said that the truly blessed person is one whose lawless deeds are forgiven, whose sins are covered, and whose sin is not held against him. True rejoicing is possible when we receive forgiveness from the Lord. Forgiveness from the Lord is possible because of Jesus' sacrificial death on the cross. Our repentance and faith in Jesus are based on the grace of God. Psalm 51 is a wonderful prayer of David, where he repents of his transgressions, iniquity, and sin. David confessed his sin and placed himself on the mercy and lovingkindness of the Lord.

ABRAHAM JUSTIFIED BY FAITH BEFORE CIRCUMCISION

Cometh this blessedness then upon the circumcision only, or upon the uncircumcision also? (Romans 4:9).

To better understand this passage, we must understand the importance the Jews gave to circumcision. No matter a person's lineage, he was not a Jew if he remained uncircumcised. Such were not allowed to eat the Passover if they had not been circumcised.

For we say that faith was reckoned to Abraham for righteousness. How was it then reckoned? When he was in circumcision, or in uncircumcision? Not in circumcision, but in uncircumcision (Romans 4:9b–10).

The objector to Paul's argument might concede that Abraham had believed and obeyed God. But they would argue that Abraham had been circumcised. However, Abraham obeyed God's call on his life, as recorded in Genesis 15. It was not until Genesis 17 that Abraham was circumcised. Therefore, circumcision was not the way to a right relationship with God; it was faith.

And he received the sign of circumcision, a seal of the righteousness of the faith which he had yet being uncircumcised: that he might be the father of all them that believe, though they be not circumcised; that righteousness might be imputed unto them also: and the father of circumcision to them who are not of the circumcision only, but who also walk in the steps of that faith of our father Abraham, which he had being yet uncircumcised (Romans 4:11–12).

Abraham is the father of the uncircumcised who believe and the circumcised who believe. Circumcision was both a sign and a seal. As a sign, it labeled Abraham as righteous, and it was a seal that proved his righteousness.

For Abraham, circumcision was a sign that sealed his dedication to the Lord. An old saying indicated a document or contract had been confirmed: signed, sealed, and delivered. It meant the contract was properly signed, sealed to prove its authenticity, and then delivered to the proper authority. Abraham had signed, sealed, and delivered his life to the Lord.

So Abraham is the father of all who walk in the steps of faith, whether circumcised or not.

THE PROMISE GRANTED THROUGH FAITH

For the promise, that he should be the heir of the world, was not to Abraham, or to his seed, through the law, but through the righteousness of faith. For if they which are of the law be heirs, faith is made void, and the promise made of none effect: Because the law worketh wrath: for where no law is, there is no transgression (Romans 4:13–15).

God's promise to Abraham was not made through the law, but through the righteousness of faith. The promise is recorded in Genesis 17:4: "As for Me, behold My covenant is with you, and you shall be a father of many nations" (NKJV). God promised that Abraham would become a great nation. This was God's grace at work in response to Abraham's faith. The Israelites were the primary descendants of Abraham, but Abraham was also the father of Ishmael and the Arab nations.

Paul used the Greek word for promise, which means an unconditional promise made from a generous heart. God's gracious promise was based on God's grace and Abraham's faith. Also, at this point, God changed Abram's name to Abraham. Abram means exalted father, and Abraham means father of many.

The promise was not made through the law. The consequences of the law are an awareness of sin and transgression ("stepping over the boundaries"). Additionally, the law would cancel the promise because faith is made void (14–15).

Therefore it is of faith, that it might be by grace; to the end the promise might be sure to all the seed; not to that only which is of the law, but to that also which is of the faith of Abraham; who is the father of us all (Romans 4:16).

As he does so often, Paul writes a long sentence. He is concluding this part of his debate with his objector. God's promises to Abraham were based on Abraham's faith and God's grace. Since the promise is based on faith, it is available to Abraham's descendants by blood and to those of Abraham's faith. The promise is not based on keeping the law or any religious ritual, like circumcision, but on faith like Abraham.

(As it is written, I have made thee a father of many nations,) before him whom he believed, even God, who quickeneth the dead, and calleth those things which be not as though they were. Who against hope believed in hope, that he might become the father of many nations, according to that which was spoken, So shall thy seed be (Romans 4:17–18).

Abraham received this promise when he was one hundred years old, and Sarah was ninety (Genesis 17:17). Abraham believed God's promise to give him a son because he believed God could give life to the dead and create life out of nothing. This promise was beyond any reasoning of hope, but Abraham believed God's promises were true: "contrary to hope, in hope he believed" (18). Abraham believed God could make the impossible possible.

If everything depended on us, we would become discouraged. On our own, we can accomplish little for the kingdom of God. But if we are alive in Christ, we can accomplish all the Lord has for us to do. Paul wrote: "I can do all things through Christ who strengthens me" (Philippians 4:13 NKJV).

And being not weak in faith, he considered not his own body now dead, when he was about an hundred years old, neither yet the deadness of Sarah's womb: He staggered not at the promise of God through unbelief; but was strong in faith, giving glory to God; and being fully persuaded that, what he had promised, he was able also to perform. And therefore it was imputed to him for righteousness (Romans 4:19–22).

Even though Abraham was physically beyond having a child, he based his hope on God's promise. Sarah had no children and, at her age, was well past childbearing age. Abraham did not waver but, by his faith, believed the God who made this promise could carry it out. Abraham gave glory to God. This means he was convinced God was powerful enough to keep His promise. Again, the faith of Abraham was accounted to him for righteousness (22).

Now it was not written for his sake alone, that it was imputed to him; but for us also, to whom it shall be imputed, if we believe on him that raised up Jesus our Lord from the dead; who was delivered for our offences, and was raised again for our justification (Romans 4:23–25).

God did not have Abraham's faith written in the Scripture just for Abraham to be remembered. The events of Abraham's life of faith are written as an example to all people and written for all who believe in God, who raised Jesus our Lord from the dead. Abraham believed God could bring life from death.

We follow in Abraham's footsteps when we believe God raised Jesus from the dead. Jesus died as a willing sacrifice for our offenses, and He was raised from the dead so we can be made right with God. Because Jesus was raised from the dead, we know all who have put their faith in Jesus will also be raised to walk in the newness of life (Romans 6:4).

CHAPTER 5

FAITH TRIUMPHS IN TIMES OF TROUBLE

The first five verses of this chapter give one of the most powerful theological passages in the Bible. Paul mentions the trinity: God and the Lord Jesus Christ in verse 1 and the Holy Spirit in verse 5.

Paul also lists most of the great descriptive words of the gospel: justified, faith, peace, access, grace, rejoice, hope, God's glory, perseverance, character, and love.

JUSTIFIED BY FAITH

Therefore being justified by faith, we have peace with God through our Lord Jesus Christ (Romans 5:1).

Paul had given his argument about salvation for the Jews and Gentiles. After his argument, he provides his summary statement. Paul maintains we are made right with God by faith. We are saved by believing and obeying Jesus as Lord. All who do will then have peace with God. Peace is not a feel-good emotion but the absence of hostilities. We are no longer enemies of God but have become a child of the King.

Paul wrote, "For He Himself is our peace, who has made both one, and broken down the middle wall of separation, having abolished in His flesh the enmity … and that He might reconcile them both to God in one body through the cross, thereby putting to death the enmity" (Ephesians 2:14–16 NKJV).

Peace was established with God because of the sacrificial death of

Jesus Christ on the cross. All people, Jew and Gentile alike, can have peace with God through Jesus, who grants us access to God.

By whom also we have access by faith into this grace wherein we stand, and rejoice in hope of the glory of God (Romans 5:2).

The word "access" means an invitation to enter the king's presence. Because of faith in the Lord Jesus Christ, a person is invited into the presence of the Lord God Almighty. A believer can enter into His grace — His unmerited favor — and remain there. Stand means our position in grace is established by faith in Jesus as Lord.

Believers can rejoice. Rejoice can be translated as boast, which means we can publicly celebrate our new position with Christ. We are adopted into the family of God, and we can call God Abba, Father (Romans 8:15).

Believers also have hope. This hope is not wishful thinking but instead found in the reality of the Word of God. As sinners, we were enemies of God, but the death of Jesus on the cross brought us to God. God's grace saves us through faith. Our hope is one day to stand in the presence ("glory") of God.

And not only so, but we glory in tribulations also: knowing that tribulation worketh patience (Romans 5:3).

Paul believed there was more to this personal relationship of faith in God. We can even boast or glory in tribulations. The word translated tribulations can be translated as pressure or stress. We face many pressures in life, such as family relationships, jobs, economic issues, sorrow, loneliness, unpopularity, and persecution. The evil world tries to press us into its mold, urging us constantly to conform. But Paul admonished the church in Rome, "And do not be conformed to this world but be transformed by the renewing of your mind" (Romans 12:2 NKJV).

Pressure produces perseverance. The word perseverance can be translated as fortitude. This attitude is not passive but works to overcome trouble and tribulations. In this life, all is not sweetness and light. Believers face trouble, but we must take the attitude of fortitude and keep on with Jesus.

And patience, experience; and experience, hope (Romans 5:4).

The word character comes from a Greek word concerning refining metal by fire to remove impurities. I grew up in the small town of Rockwood, Tennessee. Immediately after the Civil War, Northerners, familiar with the area, returned to begin the first Bessemer process of refining iron ore in the South. The metal ore was heated in a furnace, causing the slag or impurities to rise. The slag was removed, cooled, and dumped outside the furnace. Purified iron resulted. As we cling to the Lord through life's pressures and heat, we are cleansed from impurities and grow stronger. Our character has been refined by fire. And character produces hope.

And hope maketh not ashamed; because the love of God is shed abroad in our hearts by the Holy Ghost which is given unto us (Romans 5:5).

This hope is not wishful thinking but is based on God's eternal love. Believers will not be disappointed in the outcome of their lives because their hope is anchored in God. God's love is abundant. His love is poured out. There is no trickle-down effect because God's love is abundant. The proof of the love of God is that He gives believers His presence through the Holy Spirit.

CHRIST AS OUR SUBSTITUTE

For when we were yet without strength, in due time Christ died for the ungodly (Romans 5:6).

Without strength denotes that we were incapable of saving ourselves while in our sin. A drowning man cannot grab his hair and pull himself out of the water. We cannot save ourselves. Jesus died on the cross in our place and took upon Himself the penalty for our sins. Jesus died for us, the ungodly.

For scarcely for a righteous man will one die: yet peradventure for a good man some would even dare to die. But God commendeth his love toward us, in that, while we were yet sinners, Christ died for us (Romans 5:7–8).

The truth that Jesus died for us is the final proof of God's love. Jesus said, "For God so loved the world that He gave His only begotten Son that whoever believes in Him should not perish but have everlasting life" (John 3:16 NKJV).

It would be rare for someone to die in the place of a righteous person. Maybe someone would risk their lives for a good person, but the powerful love of God was displayed when Jesus died for all sinners.

JUSTIFIED BY HIS BLOOD

Much more then, being now justified by his blood, we shall be saved from wrath through him. For if, when we were enemies, we were reconciled to God by the death of his Son, much more, being reconciled, we shall be saved by his life. And not only so, but we also joy in God through our Lord Jesus Christ, by whom we have now received the atonement (Romans 5:9–11).

Jesus died in our place and justified us (made us right with God) by His death on the cross, saving us from the judgmental wrath of God. We were the enemies of God. All people since Adam have rebelled against God. "All we like sheep have gone astray; we have turned, every one, to his own way; and the Lord has laid on Him the iniquity of us all" (Isaiah 53:6 NKJV).

We were brought to God or reconciled through Jesus' death for our sins on the cross. Jesus made peace with God for us through His blood. The resurrection of Jesus provided the way for our resurrection to eternal life.

In addition, Paul said we can rejoice in God when we trust Jesus as Lord because, through Jesus, we are restored to the full fellowship of God's presence. The whole saving process — the coming of Christ and His death, burial, and resurrection — is evidence of God's love. Jesus came to show that God is and always has been love.

DEATH IN ADAM, LIFE IN CHRIST

Wherefore, as by one man sin entered into the world, and death by sin; and so death passed upon all men, for that all have sinned: (For until the law sin was in the world: but sin is not imputed when there is no law. Nevertheless death reigned from Adam to Moses, even over them that had not sinned after the similitude of Adam's transgression, who is the figure of him that was to come. But not as the offence, so also is the free gift. For if through the offence of one many be dead, much more the grace of God, and the gift by grace, which is by one man, Jesus Christ, hath abounded unto many. And not as it was by one that sinned, so is the gift: for the judgment was by one to condemnation, but the free gift is of many offences unto justification. For if by one man's offence death reigned by one; much more they which receive abundance of grace and of the gift of righteousness shall reign in life by one, Jesus Christ.) Therefore as by the offence of one judgment came upon all men to condemnation; even so by the righteousness of one the free gift came upon all men unto justification of life. For as by one man's disobedience many were made sinners, so by the obedience of one shall many be made righteous. Moreover the law entered, that the offence might abound. But where sin abounded, grace did much more abound: That as sin hath reigned unto death, even so might grace reign through righteousness unto eternal life by Jesus Christ our Lord (Romans 5:12–21).

This passage has an essential influence on understanding God's plan of salvation. However, it is difficult for many to understand. Paul begins a sentence in verse 12 but does not finish it. Paul then begins another long sentence that runs from verse 13 through verse 17.

A summary of what Paul said is that the sin of Adam infected all people with sin and then separated them from God. But because of God's grace through the righteousness of Jesus Christ, all people can have a right relationship with God. Paul wrote in his letter to the Corinthian Christians, "For since by man came death, by Man also came the resurrection of the

dead. For as in Adam all die, even so in Christ all shall be made alive"
(1 Corinthians 15:21–22 NKJV).

Perhaps this chart will help visualize how Paul compared and
contrasted Adam and Christ.

	Adam		Christ
Verse 12–14	Death Through Sin	Verse 15	Grace
Verse 16	Judgment and Condemnation	Verse 16	Free Gift and Justification
Verse 17	Death Reigned	Verse 17	Grace and Righteousness Reign
Verse 18	Offense = Judgment	Verse 18	Righteousness = Justification
Verse 19	Disobedience = Sin	Verse 19	Obedience = Righteousness
Verse 20	Law Reveals Sin	Verse 20	Grace
Verse 21	Sin Reigned in Death	Verse 21	Grace Reigned to Eternal Life

People are hopelessly lost in sin yet can be saved by Jesus Christ.
People can be redeemed by grace from the slavery to sin through faith
in the Lord Jesus Christ. He paid the penalty for sin by His death on the
cross.

CHAPTER 6

CRUCIFIED WITH CHRIST

Again, Paul debates an imaginary opponent. He probably recalled objections he had heard from his critics. So now, he answers their objections and further explains God's amazing grace.

DEAD TO SIN, ALIVE IN CHRIST

What shall we say then? Shall we continue in sin, that grace may abound? God forbid. How shall we, that are dead to sin, live any longer therein? (Romans 6:1–2).

Paul must have been accused of teaching the false doctrine that sin makes grace more abundant (Romans 5:21–22). So, Paul's imaginary opponent asked, "Why not continue in sin?" To counter this argument, Paul declared that a believer who continues in sin would be denying their faith relationship with Jesus Christ. "God forbid" is the strongest negative phrase in biblical Greek. In Paul's estimation, the idea of a believer living in sin to receive more grace was an absolute evil. Since believers have died to sin, they should not live a sinful lifestyle.

THE PICTURE OF BAPTISM

Know ye not, that so many of us as were baptized into Jesus Christ were baptized into his death? Therefore we are buried with him by baptism into death: that like as Christ was raised up from the dead by the glory of the Father, even so we also should walk in newness of life (Romans 6:3–4).

Paul uses the picture of the believer's baptism as a sign that believers have identified with the life, death, and resurrection of Jesus Christ. The Greek word for baptism means immersion. Jesus died on the cross, was buried in a tomb, and then rose again. Believers' baptism symbolizes a person's death to their old sinful life — "buried with Jesus through baptism." Jesus' death becomes our death. When we identify with Jesus' death and burial, we also identify with His resurrection. We should then walk in newness of life. Baptism symbolizes the death, burial, and resurrection of Jesus.

NO LONGER SLAVES TO SIN

For if we have been planted together in the likeness of his death, we shall be also in the likeness of his resurrection: Knowing this, that our old man is crucified with him, that the body of sin might be destroyed, that henceforth we should not serve sin (Romans 6:5–6).

Through the outward sign of baptism, believers witness their identity in Christ and His death and resurrection. A true believer will live a new life of trust and obedience to Christ. When believers identify with Christ, they also become united together.

Paul said our old person was crucified with Christ. The old man refers to the person we were before trusting Christ. But this old nature was crucified with Christ. If a person has trusted Jesus as Savior and Lord, they become a new person in Christ. "Therefore, if anyone is in Christ, he is a new creation; old things have passed away; behold, all things have become new" (2 Corinthians 5:17 NKJV).

The results of our old self being crucified with Christ are two-fold: the sinful nature in a believer's life is done away with, and we are no longer slaves of sin. Believers are a new creation, no longer enslaved to the old sinful nature connected to Adam's sin nature.

LIVING WITH JESUS

For he that is dead is freed from sin. Now if we be dead with Christ, we believe that we shall also live with him: Knowing that Christ being raised from the dead dieth no more; death hath no more dominion over him (Romans 6:7–9).

The word "freed" is the Greek word for justification, which is a legal term. The person who has died with Christ no longer has any legal obligation in sin. They have been freed. Believers must believe they have died to sin and are alive in Christ. It is not enough to intellectually know these facts.

Jesus died once and for all for sin. Once He was resurrected, He would never die again. Death has no dominion over Him.

ALIVE IN CHRIST

For in that he died, he died unto sin once: but in that he liveth, he liveth unto God. Likewise reckon ye also yourselves to be dead indeed unto sin, but alive unto God through Jesus Christ our Lord (Romans 6:10–11).

When Jesus died on the cross, He paid the penalty for sin for all people who believe. Jesus has eternal life with the Father. Paul uses a powerful word to connect believers with the work of Christ again: likewise. Since believers have identified with Jesus Christ in His death and resurrection, they can also believe they will one day be with God.

"Reckon" is an accounting word that means "to calculate." Paul said believers died with Christ and were raised with Him. Believers' calculations should lead them to realize they are dead to sin and can resist it. Like Jesus, believers are alive to God because of the ministry of the Lord Jesus Christ.

Sin Has No Dominion

Let not sin therefore reign in your mortal body, that ye should obey it in the lusts thereof. Neither yield ye your members as instruments of unrighteousness unto sin: but yield yourselves unto God, as those that are alive from the dead, and your members as instruments of righteousness unto God. For sin shall not have dominion over you: for ye are not under the law, but under grace (Romans 6:12–14).

Paul had been writing about how believers have died and risen with Christ. Paul used the picture of baptism to illustrate a believer's new position in Christ — through grace by faith.

Now, Paul turns to a practical demand. In light of his explanation in the previous verses, it is time to act on the truth of our new position with our Savior, Jesus Christ.

Being a Christian is an emotional high and a way of life. However wonderful the feeling of being saved, we must live a changed life. Religious feeling is not the end goal. The goal is to obey our Lord Jesus Christ. Jesus called his disciples to follow Him. Our challenge is the same. We are to live a life worthy of our Lord. Sin cannot reign in our human body if we do not allow it. We don't have to obey sin. We do not have to live an unrighteous life. But why not?

When we repent of our sins and commit our lives to the Lord, we present our lives to God as being alive from the dead. If we have been saved and made alive in Jesus, we have the Holy Spirit and can resist the devil. Paul maintained sin has no dominion over us. We are no longer under the law but under grace.

We cannot satisfy the demands of the law on our own. We are under grace. Our goal is to live a life pleasing to the Lord. We are not saved by the regulations of the law but by grace through faith. We are not saved by what happened on Mt. Sinai but by what happened on Mount Calvary.

FROM SLAVES OF SIN TO SLAVES OF GOD

What then? Shall we sin, because we are not under the law, but under grace? God forbid. Know ye not, that to whom ye yield yourselves servants to obey, his servants ye are to whom ye obey; whether of sin unto death, or of obedience unto righteousness? (Romans 6:15–16).

Again, Paul was debating someone who argued that we don't need to worry about sin because of God's grace. Why not live like we want, knowing that we will be forgiven in the end? Paul answered this question by using the picture of slavery. A person who is enslaved must obey their master. If we are a slave to sin, the end is death. But if we are a slave to God, the end is life.

In Paul's time, slaves were under the total control of their masters. Since a slave was owned by his master, it was impossible to serve two masters. The believers to whom Paul wrote were once slaves to sin, but they had received God as their Master and were moving toward their home in heaven.

Paul used the human analogy of slavery so the people would understand. Paul did not like to compare the Christian life to slavery, but the picture is clear. A Christian can have no master but God. We cannot give God a part of our life and give the rest to worldly pursuits. God must have all of us or nothing. If we are determined to withhold any facet of our lives from God, we cannot be a Christian.

OBEDIENCE FROM THE HEART

But God be thanked, that ye were the servants of sin, but ye have obeyed from the heart that form of doctrine which was delivered you. Being then made free from sin, ye became the servants of righteousness. I speak after the manner of men because of the infirmity of your flesh: for as ye have yielded your members servants to uncleanness and to iniquity unto iniquity; even so now yield your members servants to righteousness unto holiness (Romans 6:17–19).

Paul said they had decided to obey the Lord Jesus Christ and His teaching freely. Baptism in the New Testament was administered to believing adults coming from Judaism or paganism. Before being baptized, they were taught all the fundamentals of the Christian life and the seriousness of their commitment to Jesus as Lord.

A person who desires to be a church member should publicly repent and confess their faith in Jesus Christ as their Lord and Savior. Early believers were taught what following Christ offered and what being a true follower of Christ demanded. Christians have the promise of eternal life and the responsibility to take up their cross and follow Jesus.

Paul pointed out the difference between the old and new life in Christ. The old life was characterized by lawlessness. Noticing the many evil and unspeakable things reported in the news every day makes us realize how depraved humanity is. That is the law of sin.

THE GIFT OF GOD

For when ye were the servants of sin, ye were free from righteousness. What fruit had ye then in those things whereof ye are now ashamed? For the end of those things is death. But now being made free from sin, and become servants to God, ye have your fruit unto holiness, and the end everlasting life. For the wages of sin is death; but the gift of God is eternal life through Jesus Christ our Lord (Romans 6:20–23).

Sin produces more sin. It is a deadly downward spiral. The fruit, the result of sin, is death. The first time we do an evil thing, we may feel remorse. But the more we do it, the easier it becomes — like taking drugs. A little sin at first might satisfy, but soon, we crave more and more. When we start down the path of sin, the path grows broader and easier to travel.

But when we seek righteousness, we honor God as Lord of our lives and respect others. A Christian would never want to use or abuse another human being in any way to gratify his lust, pleasure, or greed.

Paul closes this chapter with a great and familiar verse, using two military terms in verse 23: wage and gift. The word "wage" or "pay" was used for a soldier's regular pay. It was something he earned that could not be taken from him. "Gift" referred to a gift given to soldiers on a special occasion. So, the pay a person earns for sin is death, but the gift of God is eternal life in Christ Jesus our Lord.

Chapter 7

The Purpose of the Law

Paul argued his case for the gospel of Jesus Christ. God's plan of salvation included the sacrificial death of His Son on the cross, along with His resurrection and eventual return. God's grace was poured out because of the cross of Jesus Christ. When anyone trusts and obeys Jesus as Lord, they have His righteousness accounted to them. But the question of the Jews was, "What is the function of the law?" Paul sought to explain the place of the law in this chapter.

Freed from the Law

Know ye not, brethren, (for I speak to them that know the law,) how that the law hath dominion over a man as long as he liveth? For the woman which hath an husband is bound by the law to her husband so long as he liveth; but if the husband be dead, she is loosed from the law of her husband. So then if, while her husband liveth, she be married to another man, she shall be called an adulteress: but if her husband be dead, she is free from that law; so that she is no adulteress, though she be married to another man.

Wherefore, my brethren, ye also are become dead to the law by the body of Christ; that ye should be married to another, even to him who is raised from the dead, that we should bring forth fruit unto God. For when we were in the flesh, the motions of sins, which were by the law, did work in our members to bring forth fruit unto death. But now we are delivered from the law, that being dead wherein we were held; that we should serve in newness of spirit, and not in the oldness of the letter (Romans 7:1–6).

The basic concept of this passage is Paul's argument that death cancels the laws of contracts. Paul uses the illustration of marriage. As long as a woman's husband was alive, she could not marry another. She was considered an adulteress if she married another while her husband was alive. But if the husband died, the marriage contract was canceled, and she could marry again.

In verse 4, Paul comes to the point of his illustration. He said all believers are dead to the law, having identified with the death of Jesus on the cross. Now, believers could enter a union with another: the Lord Jesus Christ. Jesus was raised from the dead, enabling those who believed in Him to bear fruit to God. Since believers have died with Jesus, they are freed from the law. So, a believer does not marry the law but marries Christ. Christian obedience is not based on external obedience to a written code. Instead, Christian obedience to God stems from a grateful heart and a spirit devoted to Jesus Christ.

In verse 5, Paul used the phrase "in the flesh" to denote the life lived before knowing Christ. Before people trust Jesus as Savior, they may live by a set of rules or no rules at all. There is within our human nature a disposition to sin. Since Adam and Eve disobeyed God in the Garden of Eden, humanity has displayed this nature. It is our human nature apart from God.

When our human nature does not obey God, the law reveals that as sin. That a thing is forbidden by the law makes it more attractive for someone not in a personal relationship with Christ. With nothing but the law, people were hopeless. But when we believe in Jesus, our lives are not ruled by a written code. Rather, our lives are ruled by faith in Jesus Christ and the indwelling Holy Spirit. It is not law but the love of Jesus and love for Jesus that makes living with Jesus possible.

THE LAW AND SIN

What shall we say then? Is the law sin? God forbid. Nay, I had not known sin, but by the law: for I had not known lust, except the law had said, Thou shalt not covet. But sin, taking occasion by the commandment, wrought in me all manner of concupiscence. For without the law sin was dead. For I was alive without the law once: but when the commandment came, sin revived, and I died. And the commandment, which was ordained to life, I found to be unto death. For sin, taking occasion by the commandment, deceived me, and by it slew me. Wherefore the law is holy, and the commandment holy, and just, and good (Romans 7:7–12).

This is a powerful passage. Paul begins by dealing with a problematic idea concerning the law. God gave the law, which is holy, just, and good. If someone could keep the law perfectly, he would be in perfect harmony with God and others. The law was given as a guide for how to live. But at the same time, sin can enter a person's life by the law.

The law defined sin. Without the law, a person would not know sin. Something forbidden creates a desire to have it or do the forbidden thing. Adam and Eve lived in innocence in the Garden. They were commanded not to touch the forbidden tree. But the serpent came and turned that prohibition into a temptation. The fact that the fruit was forbidden made it more desirable.

Paul said, "But sin, taking occasion by the commandment, wrought in me all manner of concupiscence [evil desire]" (8). Sin seduced Paul. Deception is always an essential ingredient of sin. We may reason that we will be wealthier, happier, or more powerful if we commit that sin. We even believe we can excuse our behavior or escape the consequences of our actions. The law revealed the terrible nature of sin. Sin can even twist something good into something evil.

THE LAW AND SALVATION

Was then that which is good made death unto me? God forbid. But sin, that it might appear sin, working death in me by that which is good; that sin by the commandment might become exceeding sinful. For we know that the law is spiritual: but I am carnal, sold under sin. For that which I do I allow not: for what I would, that do I not; but what I hate, that do I. If then I do that which I would not, I consent unto the law that it is good. Now then it is no more I that do it, but sin that dwelleth in me (Romans 7:13–17).

Paul faced another question: Was what was good bringing death to him? Again, Paul answered with an emphatic no. It was sin that produced death through the good he could not do. Paul told of his experience, which is common to all human beings. He knew what was right, but he could never do it somehow. He knew what was wrong. He didn't want to do it, but he did. He felt as if there were a civil war inside of him.

The Jews believed every person had two natures — an impulse toward good and an impulse toward evil. The Jews believed the law could defeat the evil impulse inside. Paul knew that teaching. He knew a battle raged on the inside that he could not win. It is not enough to know the right thing to do because we cannot do it ourselves. Only when we are in a right relationship with Jesus Christ can we do the right thing. Without the power of Jesus Christ, we cannot live the life the Lord desires.

THE INSUFFICIENCY OF HUMAN NATURE TO SAVE

For I know that in me (that is, in my flesh) dwelleth no good thing: for to will is present with me; but how to perform that which is good I find not. For the good that I would I do not: but the evil which I would not, that I do. Now if I do that I would not, it is no more I that do it, but sin that dwelleth in me. I find then a law, that, when I would do good, evil is present with me (Romans 7:18–21).

Paul acknowledged that there was nothing good in his human nature (flesh). Even by the force of his will, he couldn't do good. He could not overcome evil even though he delighted in the law of God in his heart (22). So, the inward battle raged. The good Paul wanted to do, he could not do, and the evil he did not want to do, he did. He realized sin dwelled in him. Paul discovered a natural law. Although he willed to do good, evil was present in him.

THE CIVIL WAR

For I delight in the law of God after the inward man: But I see another law in my members, warring against the law of my mind, and bringing me into captivity to the law of sin which is in my members. O wretched man that I am! Who shall deliver me from the body of this death? I thank God through Jesus Christ our Lord. So then with the mind I myself serve the law of God; but with the flesh the law of sin (Romans 7:22–25).

Although Paul delighted in the law of God, another law warred against the law of his mind that overcame his will and made him captive to the law of sin. Paul felt like a prisoner of war in the battle for his soul.

Paul realized his wretched condition. All people are in this same position outside of Jesus Christ. Paul cried out for deliverance from this death sentence.

I can visualize Paul in great praise, shouting, "I thank God!" Paul knew his mind, will, wisdom, knowledge, and nothing of himself could conquer sin. Only through the Lord Jesus Christ can anyone be delivered from this body of death. As long as we are in human flesh, the battle continues in our choices about our actions. But the battle is the Lord's (1 Samuel 17:17). And we know that those who put their faith and trust in Jesus will win the battle. "In the world you will have tribulation; but be of good cheer, I have overcome the world" (John 16:33 NKJV).

CHAPTER 8

NO CONDEMNATION FOR THOSE IN CHRIST JESUS

This chapter is problematic for several reasons. Paul referenced things he had already discussed. He references two competing principles of life — flesh and Spirit — and also deals with the powerful image of adoption. However, the most controversial questions have arisen over the nature of God's plan of salvation.

SAVED BY CHRIST JESUS

There is therefore now no condemnation to them which are in Christ Jesus, who walk not after the flesh, but after the Spirit. For the law of the Spirit of life in Christ Jesus hath made me free from the law of sin and death. For what the law could not do, in that it was weak through the flesh, God sending his own Son in the likeness of sinful flesh, and for sin, condemned sin in the flesh: That the righteousness of the law might be fulfilled in us, who walk not after the flesh, but after the Spirit (Romans 8:1–4).

The only way out of our sinful nature is to be in Christ Jesus. Paul often used this phrase to denote that a person had entered into a saving relationship with Jesus Christ. This person was not condemned because they did not walk in the flesh but in the Spirit (1).

The word "walk" could be translated as "manner of living" or "lifestyle." The word translated "flesh" was used in several ways by Paul. Paul used it to refer to literal human flesh, but he also used it for the idea of the human viewpoint. Most often, however, Paul used it to mean sinful human nature separated from Christ.

Paul used the word Spirit twenty times in this chapter. Paul referred to the powerful Holy Spirit of God that came to dwell in the believer's life. The Holy Spirit changed a person's position from hopeless to everlasting hope in Jesus Christ.

Paul's conclusion from his argument in chapter 7 was that there was no condemnation for those in Christ Jesus. For in Christ Jesus, Paul had the Spirit of life that freed him from the law of death (1). Because human nature is weak, the law cannot save us. But God sent His Son in the likeness of sinful flesh (3). Jesus came in human nature but remained sinless. He defeated sin on the cross. Jesus was fully a man, yet He fulfilled God's law. As believers in Jesus Christ, we fulfill the law's righteous requirements because we live in the Spirit and not in the flesh (4).

ALIVE IN THE SPIRIT

For they that are after the flesh do mind the things of the flesh; but they that are after the Spirit the things of the Spirit. For to be carnally minded is death; but to be spiritually minded is life and peace. Because the carnal mind is enmity against God: for it is not subject to the law of God, neither indeed can be. So then they that are in the flesh cannot please God (Romans 8:5–8).

Some people's lives are dominated by their sinful human nature because that is the focus of their minds. But others' lives are dominated by the Spirit because the focus of their minds is the Spirit. The Spirit-controlled life becomes more like Christ as one draws closer to Christ (5).

Following the flesh leads to death, but following the Spirit leads to life and peace (6). We find true peace with God in this world and eternal life in His presence in the next.

The carnal mind is the enemy of God. Human nature, controlled by the flesh, will not and cannot keep the law of God (7). So, it is impossible for those who live only in the flesh ever to please God (8).

CHRIST IN YOU

But ye are not in the flesh, but in the Spirit, if so be that the Spirit of God dwell in you. Now if any man have not the Spirit of Christ, he is none of his. And if Christ be in you, the body is dead because of sin; but the Spirit is life because of righteousness. But if the Spirit of him that raised up Jesus from the dead dwell in you, he that raised up Christ from the dead shall also quicken your mortal bodies by his Spirit that dwelleth in you (Romans 8:9–11).

Paul turns his attention to the believers in Rome. He believed they lived in the Spirit and not in the flesh if the Spirit of God indwelled them. If anyone does not have the Spirit of Christ dwelling in them, they do not belong to Jesus (9).

Notice that Paul spoke of the Spirit, the Spirit of God, and the Spirit of Christ in verse 9. We see the unity of God expressed in the trinity of names Paul used.

Paul then spoke of the effect of the work of Jesus in our lives. The conditional "if" is important. If Christ is in us (10). This is the key truth. If Jesus is in us, our old sin life is dead, and our spirit is alive. Jesus has made us right with God. All people sinned in Adam, and death came because of sin. But all people can be saved in Jesus because, by His death, we are made right with God.

Our way to eternal life is not through good works or because we deserve it. Remember, the wages of sin is death. But if the Spirit that raised Jesus from the dead lives in us, He will also raise us from the dead (11). The person who has trusted Jesus as Savior and is indwelt by the Spirit is on the way to eternal life. Death is just a door we must walk through on the way to the presence of the Father.

ADOPTED INTO THE FAMILY OF GOD

Therefore, brethren, we are debtors, not to the flesh, to live after the flesh. For if ye live after the flesh, ye shall die: but if ye through the Spirit do mortify the deeds of the body, ye shall live. For as many as are led by the Spirit of God, they are the sons of God. For ye have not received the spirit of bondage again to fear; but ye have received the Spirit of adoption, whereby we cry, Abba, Father. The Spirit itself beareth witness with our spirit, that we are the children of God: And if children, then heirs; heirs of God, and joint-heirs with Christ; if so be that we suffer with him, that we may be also glorified together (Romans 8:12–17).

Again, Paul concluded about our living in Christ. He repeated the truth that we are debtors to God, not to our human nature, which cannot save (12). We are alive in the Spirit, but those who live for the flesh are dead spiritually (13). The true test of whether someone is a child of God is if they are led by the Spirit (14). Being led involves our active participation, relationship with the Lord, and our submissive dependence on Him.

Believers are children of God because we have received the Spirit of adoption. Adoption was a complicated and serious procedure under Roman Law. A father had total power over his family. To be adopted, a child had to pass from the absolute control of one father to another. The one adopted gained all the rights of a son by birth in the new family.

He also became an heir with the same rights as the other children. Once adopted, he was considered a new person. His past was erased. Some legal witnesses could testify about the adoption, and adopted people could never be disinherited.

Believers have been adopted into the family of God, but not because it was not our right or privilege, good works, or birthright. God's grace adopts us through faith. This was God's plan so that we can cry out Abba, Father (15). Jesus used this Aramaic word for Father (Daddy) when He prayed (Mark 14:36).

The Spirit is our witness that we are children of God, heirs of God, and joint heirs with Christ (16–17). We join Christ in His sufferings and will be glorified with Him. Peter wrote that our inheritance is based on our relationship with God, which is "incorruptible, undefiled, and reserved in heaven" (1 Peter 1:4).

Being adopted by God means we have come under His authority. Our past is canceled. We are a new person, beginning a new life in Christ. We become heirs to all the riches of God. We are joint heirs with Jesus, God's only begotten Son. We enter the family of God not because we earned it or deserved it. With His amazing love and mercy, the Father takes the lost and helpless repentant sinner, forgives her, and adopts her into His family.

A New Creation

For I reckon that the sufferings of this present time are not worthy to be compared with the glory which shall be revealed in us. For the earnest expectation of the creature waiteth for the manifestation of the sons of God. For the creature was made subject to vanity, not willingly, but by reason of him who hath subjected the same in hope, because the creature itself also shall be delivered from the bondage of corruption into the glorious liberty of the children of God. For we know that the whole creation groaneth and travaileth in pain together until now (Romans 8:18–22).

Paul has just explained the believer's relationship with Jesus using the powerful image of adoption. With adoption came the promise of being in the glorious presence of the Lord, which hope not even the world's sufferings can diminish (18).

Thinking of the future glory, Paul focuses on the created world. He realized that creation was waiting in anticipation for the end times revelation of the sons of God (19). Creation waits for the liberation from sin, which has caused death and decay. Creation was subjected to futility, but creation will be restored (20). Isaiah wrote, "For behold, I create new heavens and a new earth" (Isaiah 65:17 NKJV), and "For behold I create Jerusalem as a rejoicing" (Isaiah 65:18 NKJV). John wrote, "Now I saw a new heaven and a new earth, for the first heaven and the first earth had passed away. ... Then I, John, saw the holy city, New Jerusalem, coming down out of heaven from God" (Revelation 21:1–2 NKJV).

One day, creation will be delivered from sin's dominion, and death and decay will be over. Creation will share in the glorious liberty of the children of God (21). Paul compared the longing of creation for this future liberty to a woman's birth pains. One day, creation will be delivered (22).

Waiting for the Resurrection

And not only they, but ourselves also, which have the firstfruits of the Spirit, even we ourselves groan within ourselves, waiting for the adoption, to wit, the redemption of our body. For we are saved by hope: but hope that is seen is not hope: for what a man seeth, why doth he yet hope for? But if we hope for that we see not, then do we with patience wait for it (Romans 8:23–25).

Believers groan with labor pains, eagerly looking forward to the completion of their adoption. Believers will be united with their resurrection body and gathered before the throne of almighty God (23).

Then comes a wonderful fact: "We were saved in this hope" (24). Our human circumstance is not hopeless. Paul knew that all had sinned, but he also knew the awesome power of God to save. Life in Christ guarantees redemption and a new creation (25).

The phrase "earnest expectation" in verse 19 (NKJV) comes from a Greek word that describes someone eagerly looking for the first rays of dawn. Life for so many is a weary, defeated existence that is a battle with depression, disappointment, and discouragement. But for Paul, hope was the end result of his faith in Christ. The theme of the Christian life is hope in Christ, not despair. The Christian realizes that his end is not death but eternal life.

The Intercession of the Spirit

Likewise the Spirit also helpeth our infirmities: for we know not what we should pray for as we ought: but the Spirit itself maketh intercession for us with groanings which cannot be uttered. And he that searcheth the hearts knoweth what is the mind of the Spirit, because he maketh intercession for the saints according to the will of God. And we know that all things work together for good to them that love God, to them who are the called according to his purpose (Romans 8:26–28).

These are some of the most important verses on prayer in the Bible. Paul expressed the truth that in our human weakness, we don't even know what to pray for. But the Spirit helps us in our weakness (26). We cannot pray as we should because we do not know the future, and we do not know God's best for us. Even when we cannot find the right words, the Spirit intercedes for us. "Therefore He is also able to save to the uttermost those who come to God through Him (Jesus), since He always lives to make intercession for them" (Hebrews 7:25 NKJV). Jesus saves all those who come to the Father through Him, and He always intercedes for believers. Jesus is praying for you, and His Holy Spirit is praying with you. Paul then gave a promise from the Lord. Those who respond to the invitation of the Lord will discover God is working through all the events of their lives for their good (28). Looking back over our lives, we see the Lord has guided us through it all.

A song that meant so much to me during a difficult situation is "Through It All." For a believer, the trying circumstances of life should make us run into the arms of our heavenly Father.

Our All-Knowing God

For whom he did foreknow, he also did predestinate to be conformed to the image of his Son, that he might be the firstborn among many brethren. Moreover whom he did predestinate, them he also called: and whom he called, them he also justified: and whom he justified, them he also glorified (Romans 8:29–30).

Through the years, these verses have confused some. The overwhelming majority of the Scriptures support the truth of God's plan of redemption as summarized in John 3:16: "For God so loved the world that He gave His only begotten Son, that whoever believes in Him should not perish but have everlasting life" (NKJV).

The eleventh chapter of Hebrews, the Old Testament roll call of faith, makes it clear people in Old Testament times were saved by faith. Paul has declared repeatedly in Romans that believers are justified (made right with God) through grace by faith. That is God's plan. I don't believe Paul would suddenly change his whole description of God's plan of salvation. It is not God's plan or Paul's intention to confuse. Confusion is a tool of the devil.

Those who follow the teaching of John Calvin believe salvation is all God's choice and has nothing to do with repentance and faith. They say that God's choice causes our faith. I believe the clear message of the whole Bible is that God has chosen to save all who will come to Him in repentance and faith. Yet, Calvinists believe people are so spiritually dead that they cannot choose. If a person follows what Calvin taught, they must accept that God determined before time who would go to heaven and who would go to hell. That is not the picture of the loving, merciful, gracious, and long-suffering Lord of the Bible.

We should try to understand salvation from God's perspective. Try to visualize all of history laid out like a yardstick. God's creation of everything would be at one end of the yardstick. The return of Christ and the final judgment would be at the other end. God is not bound by time. Imagine God above this yardstick of history, seeing it all from start to finish. Jesus said, "I am the Alpha and Omega, the Beginning and the End" (Revelation 1:8 NKJV).

The Lord God is also all-knowing. God knows everything about each of us. Jesus said, "But the very hairs of your head are all numbered"

(Matthew 10:30). The Lord knows our choices, but He does not determine or force us in any direction.

God had a plan for our salvation. We see it referenced in Genesis after Adam and Eve sinned. "And I will put enmity between you and the woman, and between your seed and her Seed; He shall bruise your head, and you shall bruise His heel" (Genesis 3:15 NKJV). This is God's first revelation of His plan to defeat Satan by the work of His Son Jesus.

The Bible reveals more and more of God's plan until the height of His revelation is the coming of His Son to earth in the flesh. Jesus died on the cross for our sins, was buried, and rose again so that all who believe in Him can have everlasting life (John 3:16–18).

At the end, the Bible says, "That at the name of Jesus every knee should bow, of those in heaven, and those on the earth, and those under the earth, and that every tongue should confess that Jesus Christ is Lord, to the glory of God the Father" (Philippians 2:10–11 NKJV). Those who would not believe and acknowledge Jesus as Lord before will one day have to proclaim that Jesus is Lord.

So let's examine these verses in the light of the whole Word of God.

The closing phrase of Romans 8:28 is "to those who are called according to His purpose." God chose Israel for a purpose. They were to be His witnesses to the world. This calling did not mean they were all saved. Time after time, many failed, rebelled, worshiped idols, and were destroyed. We see this cycle of repentance and rebellion clearly in Judges.

God called Moses to lead the children of Israel out of Egyptian slavery. Many of the prominent people of faith in the Old Testament were called out at a particular time to fulfill God's purpose for Israel to be faithful to God and to be His witnesses to the world. "Have I not told you from time to time, and declared it? You are my witnesses, is there a God besides Me? Indeed, there is no other Rock; I know not one" (Isaiah 44:8 NKJV).

Paul speaks of those God "foreknew" (29). We have already stated that God knows everything. His will and perfect plan are for all people to conform to the image of His Son. "The Lord is ... not willing that any should perish but that all should come to repentance" (2 Peter 3:9 NKJV). "For God so loved the world ... that whoever believes in Him should not perish but have everlasting life" (John 3:16 NKJV). The invitation is open to all. Jesus commands His disciples to "Go therefore and make disciples of all the nations" (Matthew 28:19 NKJV).

According to Strong's Concordance, the Greek word for "predestined" (29) means "to mark out beforehand" or "to establish one's boundary or one's limits beforehand." Our word "horizon" derives from this word. God has fixed the believer's horizon. God's plan is for believers to conform to His Son's image. That process will be completed in our destination, which is heaven.

Predestined is in the past tense. From God's perspective, He sees and knows the result of His process of redemption and salvation. In Revelation, John wrote of his heavenly vision. God revealed to John that all the world will conclude to fulfill God's plan of salvation for believers. In Revelation 22:17, John recorded this invitation: "And the Spirit and the bride say, 'Come!' And let him who hears say, 'Come!' And let him who thirsts come. Whoever desires, let him take the water of life freely" (NKJV).

Paul mentions those God called (30). In the Old Testament, God called Israel to be His witnesses. "For you are a holy people to the Lord you God, and the Lord has chosen you to be a people for Himself, a special treasure above all the peoples who are on the face of the earth" (Deuteronomy 14:2 NKJV).

Peter said to the church, "But you are a chosen generation, a royal priesthood, a holy nation. His own special people, that you may proclaim the praise of Him who called you out of darkness into His marvelous light, who once were not a people but are now the people of God, who had not obtained mercy but now have obtained mercy" (1 Peter 2:9–10 NKJV). Peter quotes Isaiah 28:16. Peter also said, "Therefore to you who believe,

He is precious" (1 Peter 2:7 NKJV).

Paul wrote about Israel and the church: "That Gentiles ... have attained to righteousness, even the righteousness of faith," but that "Israel ... has not attained the law of righteousness." Why? Because they did not seek it by faith (Romans 9:30–32 NKJV).

We do have a choice. Moses challenged Israel with the following words: "I call heaven and earth as witnesses today against you, that I have set before you, life and death, blessing and cursing; therefore choose life; that both you and your descendants may live; that you may love the Lord your God, that you may obey His voice, and that you may cling to Him, for He is your life" (Deuteronomy 30:19–20 NKJV).

Joshua challenged Israel by saying, "Choose for yourselves this day whom you will serve ... But as for me and my house, we will serve the Lord" (Joshua 24:14–15 NKJV).

Jesus called Matthew: "As Jesus passed on from there, He saw a man named Matthew sitting at the tax office. And He said to him 'Follow Me.' So he arose and followed Him" (Matthew 9:9 NKJV).

Elijah challenged all the people of Israel gathered on Mount Carmel: "How long will you falter between two opinions? If the Lord is God, follow Him; but if Baal, follow him" (1 Kings 18:21 NKJV). Later, the people realized the Lord was God when fire came from heaven and consumed Elijah's offering.

God's plan is seen in His perfect will: that all have the opportunity to be saved. God's plan began with His perfect love that all who respond to God's gracious invitation in repentance and faith in Jesus are justified and will one day be glorified in His presence.

God's Everlasting Love

What shall we then say to these things? If God be for us, who can be against us? He that spared not his own Son, but delivered him up for us all, how shall he not with him also freely give us all things? Who shall lay any thing to the charge of God's elect? It is God that justifieth. Who is he that condemneth? It is Christ that died, yea rather, that is risen again, who is even at the right hand of God, who also maketh intercession for us (Romans 8:31–34).

How do we respond to all the Lord has done for us (31)? Jesus came into this world. He lived. He taught. He died on the cross. He rose again. God did all of this. We did not. We received this gospel of love by faith. Grace, forgiveness, and salvation all came from the Lord. However, a person can refuse God's call and, by sinful disobedience, destroy the plan of God for their lives.

How have you responded to what God has done for you? Paul then asked a second question: If God is on our side, who can be victorious over us? The obvious answer is nothing, and no one can overcome a person who is in Christ.

The great love of God was manifested in that God did not spare His own Son but allowed Him to die for us all (32). Since God has demonstrated His great love in such a powerful way, He will freely give us all things. In another epistle, Paul said, "And my God shall supply all your needs according to His riches in glory in Christ Jesus" (Philippians 4:19).

God has acquitted us. So, who can sit in judgment over us and condemn us? The Judge of all people is Jesus Christ, but He does not condemn believers. Instead, Jesus is at the right hand of God, interceding for us. Paul said four things about Jesus. He died, He rose again, He is at the right hand of God, and He is making intercession for us (34). Jesus is the Judge, and He is our defense attorney, pleading our case. No one can overturn our acquittal verdict at the judgment seat of Christ.

Paul mentions God's elect (33). The word "elect" does not refer to salvation. In Strong's Concordance, the word means "chosen for a purpose." God elects or chooses people for a specific purpose. I believe

God chose me to be a preacher of the gospel. When I was eighteen, God called me to preach. God chose or elected Israel to be His witnesses. God has chosen or elected the church, all true believers, to be His witnesses. We are challenged to take up our cross and follow Him.

Nothing Can Separate

Who shall separate us from the love of Christ? Shall tribulation, or distress, or persecution, or famine, or nakedness, or peril, or sword? As it is written, For thy sake we are killed all the day long; we are accounted as sheep for the slaughter. Nay, in all these things we are more than conquerors through him that loved us. For I am persuaded, that neither death, nor life, nor angels, nor principalities, nor powers, nor things present, nor things to come, nor height, nor depth, nor any other creature, shall be able to separate us from the love of God, which is in Christ Jesus our Lord (Romans 8:35–39).

One of the most encouraging passages for believers in the New Testament is found in these verses. Paul begins by listing several of the most severe causes of problems in this life. Paul's first word was "tribulation." This could be any affliction, whether hardship or health problem. Distress could refer to any mental anxiety or worry. The rest of Paul's list of things we may face in this life has obvious meanings: persecution, famine, nakedness, peril, or sword. The world may be falling apart. Our world may be crumbling around us, but none of these things can separate us from the love of Christ (35).

Paul quoted Psalm 44:22 to back up his statements about the tribulations we may face. But then He gives us one of the great promises of Scripture: "We are more than conquerors through him that loved us" (37). Because of Jesus, we will overcome all these things.

In verses 38–39, Paul makes another terrible list of mainly spiritual forces that may come against us. Paul was convinced that neither life nor death could separate us from Christ. We can live and die in Christ. Death is just walking through a door that Jesus has opened into the presence of God.

Neither angels, principalities, nor powers can separate us from the love of God. I think Paul was referring to Satan and the other fallen angels who rebelled against God. The term principalities and powers was a term Paul used to describe the forces of evil. We see this in another of his epistles: "Having disarmed principalities and powers, He made a spectacle of them, triumphing over them in it" (Colossians 2:15 NKJV).

Paul said nothing in this age or the age to come could separate us from the love of God. Nothing in time can sever us from the love of Christ (38).

Height and depth are astrological terms. The ancient world, and some today, believed that the stars controlled their life and their destiny. To them, our future is sealed by the star we were born under. Height was when a star was at its highest point, and its influence was the strongest. Depth was when a star was at its lowest point and waiting to rise and exert some influence over people's lives. However, the rising and the setting of stars cannot separate us from God's love.

Nothing in God's creation can separate a person from His love (39). These promises should remove any uncertainty or fear we might have. Jesus is Lord over all, so why should we fear? This powerful chapter should be an encouragement to all believers.

CHAPTER 9

THE PROBLEM OF JESUS

In chapters 9-11, Paul deals with the difficult problems believers face: the question about the Jews. They were God's chosen people, and yet when Jesus came into the world, they rejected and crucified Him. "He came to His own, and His own did not receive Him" (John 1:11 NKJV). How can we explain God's people crucifying Jesus?

ISRAEL'S REJECTION OF JESUS

I say the truth in Christ, I lie not, my conscience also bearing me witness in the Holy Ghost, that I have great heaviness and continual sorrow in my heart. For I could wish that myself were accursed from Christ for my brethren, my kinsmen according to the flesh: Who are Israelites; to whom pertaineth the adoption, and the glory, and the covenants, and the giving of the law, and the service of God, and the promises; whose are the fathers, and of whom as concerning the flesh Christ came, who is over all, God blessed for ever. Amen (Romans 9:1–5).

Paul tried to explain the Jews' rejection of Jesus. He was not angry with the Jews but broken hearted by their rejection. He longed for his people to be saved (1–2). He was even willing to take their place if it would mean their salvation (3). The word "accursed" is *anathema* in Greek, meaning "under the ban." This was the idea of utter destruction.

As a Jew, Paul knew the privileges of being God's chosen people. God adopted them (Exodus 4:22). Israel had the glory. Many times in the history of Israel, God's divine light had visited His people. Israel had the covenants. God initiated agreements with Israel. There was a covenant with Noah, Abraham and his descendants, and the people at Mt. Sinai.

The most essential covenant was the new covenant in Christ Jesus. Israel had the law. God told them what He expected of them, and they could not plead ignorance of God's will or plan. Israel had the service of God. The Jews had the Temple and synagogues to worship God in. They were allowed to approach God in worship. Israel had the promises. Israel was to be obedient and faithful to all that God told them through His prophets and spokesman. God made them promises if they were faithful (4).

Israel had the fathers. They had the history and tradition of many faithful servants of God. This should have inspired and guided their lives.

Through Israel, the promised Messiah came. Jesus, the Messiah, is over all and is the eternally blessed God (5). The great sorrow was that Israel, despite all these privileges and advantages, rejected Jesus when He came, thus rejecting God's love.

ISRAEL'S REJECTION AND GOD'S PLAN

Not as though the word of God hath taken none effect. For they are not all Israel, which are of Israel: Neither, because they are the seed of Abraham, are they all children: but, In Isaac shall thy seed be called. That is, they which are the children of the flesh, these are not the children of God: but the children of the promise are counted for the seed. For this is the word of promise, At this time will I come, and Sarah shall have a son. And not only this; but when Rebecca also had conceived by one, even by our father Isaac; (For the children being not yet born, neither having done any good or evil, that the purpose of God according to election might stand, not of works, but of him that calleth); It was said unto her, The elder shall serve the younger. As it is written, Jacob have I loved, but Esau have I hated (Romans 9:6–13).

Just because the Jews rejected and had Jesus crucified does not mean they defeated God's plan. Paul knew that God's plan was working (6). Some Jews accepted Jesus: "But as many as received Him, to them He gave the right to become children of God, to those who believe in His name" (John 1:12 NKJV). All the early followers of Jesus, including the apostles and Paul, were Jews.

Paul made another point. Just because a person is a descendant of Abraham does not automatically make them the children of the promise (9:7–9). Jesus said, "And do not think to yourselves, 'We have Abraham as our father.' For I say to you that God is able to raise up children to Abraham from these stones" (Matthew 3:9 NKJV).

After the great contest on Mt. Carmel between God's prophet Elijah and the false priests and prophets of Baal, Elijah told God, "I alone am left" (1 Kings 19:14 NKJV). After God had given Elijah some tasks to do, God revealed to Elijah: "Yet I have reserved seven thousand in Israel, all whose knees have not bowed to Baal, and every mouth that has not kissed him" (1 Kings 19:18 NKJV). This is just one example of how a remnant always remained faithful. This remnant was the true Israel.

The promise's basis was the covenant God made with Abraham and his descendants. Israel did not earn or deserve this standing with God. God called them to be His witnesses. God called Abraham, and Abraham responded in faith. "By faith Abraham obeyed when he was called to go out to the place which he would receive as an inheritance. And he went out, not knowing where he was going" (Hebrews 11:8 NKJV). "By faith Sarah herself also received strength to conceive seed, and she bore a child when she was past the age, because she judged Him faithful who had promised" (Hebrews 11:11 NKJV). Abraham and Sarah followed the Lord, trusted in Him, and received a son in their old age (9).

God also gave sons to Rebecca and Isaac (10–13). God, knowing the future, knew He would one day meet Jacob at Bethel (Genesis 32:24). God would also change his name from Jacob (deceiver) to Israel (Prince with God) (Genesis 32:28).

God blessed Esau and made him the father of a nation. Yet God called Jacob to be in the line of the promise (11). So, again, Paul declared it is not our works, but it is according to God's purpose and plan (11). God knew Jacob would respond obediently to Him so that the line would go through Jacob as God's chosen people (12).

Esau settled in Edom, did not worship the Lord, and was rejected by God (13). Malachi recorded the downfall of Esau and condemned the false worship of Israel (Malachi 1:6–8). The prophet called for Israel to repent (1:9–11) and announced judgment on them (2:1–4).

But God reaffirmed His covenant with Israel and reminded Israel what the covenant meant (Malachi 2:5–7). God's desire is for us to be faithful. God's plan had been set in motion, and our sin and rejection will not defeat it.

ISRAEL'S REJECTION AND GOD'S JUSTICE

What shall we say then? Is there unrighteousness with God? God forbid. For he saith to Moses, I will have mercy on whom I will have mercy, and I will have compassion on whom I will have compassion. So then it is not of him that willeth, nor of him that runneth, but of God that sheweth mercy. For the scripture saith unto Pharaoh, Even for this same purpose have I raised thee up, that I might shew my power in thee, and that my name might be declared throughout all the earth. Therefore hath he mercy on whom he will have mercy, and whom he will he hardeneth (Romans 9:14–18).

God's will *will* be done. His will is not based on a person working to achieve merit with Him to put Him in a person's debt. It has nothing to do with a person deserving grace. However, that does not make God unjust (14). God plans to show mercy as He wills. It depends not on our will or effort but on God's grace (15–16). The Jews thought they could earn God's

THE PROBLEM OF JESUS

favor by keeping the law and other rules and traditions.

Paul then used the illustration of Pharaoh. He was a wicked ruler who did not believe in God and held the children of Israel as slaves in Egypt. Eleven times in Exodus, Pharaoh hardened his heart and would not let the Israelites leave. God confirmed the condition of Pharaoh's heart. Eight times, the Scripture records that God hardened Pharaoh's heart. The Lord had said, "My Spirit shall not strive with man forever" (Genesis 6:3 NKJV).

There comes a point when God confirms a sinner's rebellion. "Wherefore God also gave them up to uncleanness through the lusts of their own hearts, to dishonour their own bodies between themselves: Who changed the truth of God into a lie, and worshipped and served the creature more than the Creator, who is blessed for ever" (Romans 1:24–25; see also Romans 1:26–32).

God's purpose was: "And the Egyptians shall know that I am the Lord, when I stretch out My hand on Egypt and bring out the children of Israel from among them" (Exodus 7:5 NKJV). God cannot do anything which contradicts His own nature or that breaks His own laws.

GOD IS THE CREATOR

Thou wilt say then unto me, Why doth he yet find fault? For who hath resisted his will? Nay but, O man, who art thou that repliest against God? Shall the thing formed say to him that formed it, Why hast thou made me thus? Hath not the potter power over the clay, of the same lump to make one vessel unto honour, and another unto dishonour? What if God, willing to shew his wrath, and to make his power known, endured with much longsuffering the vessels of wrath fitted to destruction: And that he might make known the riches of his glory on the vessels of mercy, which he had afore prepared unto glory (Romans 9:19–23).

The objector in Paul's debate raised another question. Since God is in total control, why blame people when they try to resist His will (19)? How can God judge people for being unfaithful sinners if He controls history? History is His story, so how can He blame people who reject Him? This reasoning placed all of the blame on God since He is in charge.

Paul used the illustration of a potter working with clay. Paul may have been inspired by Jeremiah's experience with the potter (Jeremiah 18:1–6). Of course, there is a difference between a person and a ball of clay. Clay is a thing. It cannot question, argue, think, or feel. God does not make some people to destroy them. That would be what an evil tyrant would do, not a loving Father. The fundamental truth of the gospel is that God does not treat us like a lump of clay. God created us (Genesis 1:26–27) and calls us to be His witnesses in the world.

When I was eighteen, the Lord called me to preach. I didn't know all that the call of God in my life would involve or where it would take me. But that call is just as real now as it was over six decades ago.

It was a mind-numbing experience for Paul when God's people rejected and crucified their Messiah. Yet, people today still reject Jesus. Years ago, when visiting evangelistically door to door in our community, I asked a man, "If you were to die tonight, are you sure you would go to heaven?" The man bluntly replied, "No, I would go to hell!" There was no remorse, fear, or shame.

Paul had already said, "And we know that all things work together for good to those who love God, to those who are the called according to His purpose" (Romans 8:28 NKJV). God can use evil situations and bring good out of them. In Isaiah 53 and other "Suffering Servant" passages, Isaiah foretold the suffering of the Messiah. Jesus said, "And I, if I am lifted up from the earth, will draw all peoples to Myself" (John 12:32 NKJV). Through the agony of His suffering and death, Jesus made possible our salvation. God brought the greatest good even out of the suffering of His only begotten Son.

OLD TESTAMENT QUOTATIONS

Even us, whom he hath called, not of the Jews only, but also of the Gentiles? As he saith also in Osee, I will call them my people, which were not my people; and her beloved, which was not beloved. And it shall come to pass, that in the place where it was said unto them, Ye are not my people; there shall they be called the children of the living God. Esaias also crieth concerning Israel, Though the number of the children of Israel be as the sand of the sea, a remnant shall be saved: For he will finish the work, and cut it short in righteousness: because a short work will the Lord make upon the earth. And as Esaias said before, Except the Lord of Sabaoth had left us a seed, we had been as Sodoma, and been made like unto Gomorrha (Romans 9:24–29).

Paul used quotations from the prophets Hosea and Isaiah to support his argument that it had been foretold that Israel would reject their Messiah and that the message would go out to the Gentiles (Hosea 2:23, 1:10, Isaiah 10:22–23). However, a remnant would be saved (27). The Jews thought their good works could build up enough credit with God. The Lord would then be in their debt and would owe them salvation. Of course, we can never be good enough or do enough good deeds to earn our way into God's holy presence. When the Gentiles learned about the incredible love of God in Jesus Christ, many trusted in the love of God. The Jews tried to put God in their debt, but the Gentile believers realized the amazing grace of God and trusted Jesus as Lord and Savior.

CHRIST, THE ROCK

What shall we say then? That the Gentiles, which followed not after righteousness, have attained to righteousness, even the righteousness which is of faith. But Israel, which followed after the law of righteousness, hath not attained to the law of righteousness. Wherefore? Because they sought it not by faith, but as it were by the works of the law. For they stumbled at that stumblingstone; As it is written, Behold, I lay in Sion a stumblingstone and rock of offence: and whosoever believeth on him shall not be ashamed (Romans 9:30–33).

Paul contrasted the two ways of approaching God. The Jewish way was to make themselves righteous by strictly obeying the law. They did not go the way of faith but of the law (31). The Gentiles attained righteousness by faith (30).

In the Old Testament, several references are made to the stone. Genesis 49:24 describes God as the Shepherd and Stone of Israel. Isaiah 28:10 states that God will lay in Zion a foundation stone, a precious cornerstone. In Daniel 2:34–35, 44–45, Daniel prophesied of a stone that would crush worldly empires. Psalm 118:22 tells of a stone that builders would reject, but it would become the chief cornerstone. Jesus quoted Psalm 118:22 and applied it to Himself (Matthew 21:42). Christians in the early church realized these references described Jesus.

Paul quoted Isaiah 8:14 and 28:16. We can also see the idea of the stone found in Acts 4:11, Ephesians 2:20, and 1 Peter 2:4–6. God sent His Son Jesus into the world to be the Savior and Lord over all. When a person trusts Jesus as Lord and Savior, the stone becomes a stone of salvation for them. But if a person chooses to rebel and reject Jesus, the stone becomes condemnation. If we respond to Jesus in faith, we are saved. But if we reject Him, we will be judged unfaithful and condemned.

CHAPTER 10

CHRIST SAVES ALL WHO BELIEVE

The conclusion from chapter 9 is that Israel is under God's wrath (9:22). Paul had told the Jews truths that were hard for them to hear and accept. The section from Romans chapter 9 to chapter 11 is a condemnation of the Jewish system of religion. Paul was not angry with them but was brokenhearted by their rejection of Jesus.

ISRAEL NEEDS THE GOSPEL

Brethren, my heart's desire and prayer to God for Israel is, that they might be saved. For I bear them record that they have a zeal of God, but not according to knowledge. For they being ignorant of God's righteousness, and going about to establish their own righteousness, have not submitted themselves unto the righteousness of God. For Christ is the end of the law for righteousness to every one that believeth (Romans 10:1–4).

Paul desired for the Jews to be saved (1). To effectively witness for Christ, we must have compassion for lost people. We must plead with them to hear and believe the gospel. We should speak the truth, but always in love. Paul acknowledged that the Jews had a zeal for God (2). However, their zeal was misguided. It was based on total obedience to the law. Their religion was a real burden. They added six hundred and thirteen Sabbath laws alone. For example, a person could not cook or carry anything that weighed more than two dried figs. Nor could they start a fire or keep one going on the Sabbath. The Jews had zeal, but their strict obedience to all their rules could not earn credit with God.

They were ignorant of God's righteousness and tried to make their way to righteousness (3). Paul again confirmed that Christ is the end of legalism. They lacked the understanding of the right way to worship God. They had not submitted or obeyed God's command to believe (Romans 1:5, 6:17, Acts 16:31). Because Jesus lived and died on the cross, people no longer have to earn God's righteousness. They can now accept God's love. People can believe in the grace, love, and mercy that God freely offers to all who believe in Jesus Christ (4).

The word "end" can mean "fulfillment." Jesus fulfilled all the requirements of the law. The law reveals sin, but the people could not keep the law. Jesus fulfilled the law and offered us His righteousness through faith in Him.

THE RIGHTEOUSNESS OF FAITH

For Moses describeth the righteousness which is of the law, That the man which doeth those things shall live by them. But the righteousness which is of faith speaketh on this wise, Say not in thine heart, Who shall ascend into heaven? (that is, to bring Christ down from above:) Or, Who shall descend into the deep? (that is, to bring up Christ again from the dead.) But what saith it? The word is nigh thee, even in thy mouth, and in thy heart: that is, the word of faith, which we preach (Romans 10:5–8).

Paul used two Scripture passages to illustrate his point. He first quoted Leviticus 18:5. This passage states that when a person does those things, he shall live by them (5). The problem is no person has ever been able to live up to the law.

The righteousness that comes by faith is explained this way: it is not our effort that brought Christ into this world or raised Him from the dead (6–7). Paul quoted from Deuteronomy 30:12–13.

Paul affirmed that the Word of God is available (8). God's Word is not distant or impossible to understand. It is near you, in your mouth and your heart, that you may do it. The word Paul was talking about is the gospel. It is the word of faith which we preach (8).

SALVATION BY FAITH

That if thou shalt confess with thy mouth the Lord Jesus, and shalt believe in thine heart that God hath raised him from the dead, thou shalt be saved. For with the heart man believeth unto righteousness; and with the mouth confession is made unto salvation. For the scripture saith, Whosoever believeth on him shall not be ashamed. For there is no difference between the Jew and the Greek: for the same Lord over all is rich unto all that call upon him. For whosoever shall call upon the name of the Lord shall be saved (Romans 10:9–13).

Paul then shares the essential truths of the gospel. First, a person must confess or profess that Jesus is Lord. The word "Lord" was the usual title for the Roman emperor. It was also the title of the Greek gods. When the Greek translation of the Hebrew Scriptures was made, the word "LORD" was used whenever the Hebrew name for God was used. It was the name God revealed to Moses from the burning bush: Yahweh (Exodus 3:14). To confess Jesus as Lord meant a person believed He is God's Son, our Savior. It meant giving Jesus the supreme place in a person's life.

We must also confess that God raised Jesus from the dead. The resurrection is an essential belief. A Christian must believe that Jesus lived and died and that he rose from the dead and is alive forever. A person must not just know about Christ; he must know Christ. By believing and confessing these truths, we are saved (9).

Believing in our hearts opens the door to righteousness, and confessing with our mouths opens the door to salvation (10). To be a Christian, we believe and declare to others whose side we are on. There is no place for secret disciples or non-committed Christians. These categories won't pass

God's judgment.

Paul confirmed that the way to God is open to everybody. In verse 11, he quotes Isaiah 28:16: "Whosoever believeth on him shall not be ashamed." This is true whether a person is a Jew or a Gentile. The Lord over all is gracious to all who call on Him (12). Then, in verse 13, Paul quotes Joel 2:32: "That whoever calls on the name of the Lord will be saved" (NKJV). The promise of salvation is for everyone. The word "whoever" means "all."

Paul appeals to the Jews to turn from legalism and accept salvation by grace through faith in the Lord Jesus Christ. Paul pleaded with the Jews to look to the prophets, who declared that faith is open to all and the only way to God.

Faith Comes by Hearing the Word of God

How then shall they call on him in whom they have not believed? and how shall they believe in him of whom they have not heard? and how shall they hear without a preacher? And how shall they preach, except they be sent? as it is written, How beautiful are the feet of them that preach the gospel of peace, and bring glad tidings of good things! But they have not all obeyed the gospel. For Esaias saith, Lord, who hath believed our report? So then faith cometh by hearing, and hearing by the word of God (Romans 10:14-17).

In the previous section of his letter, Paul says the way to God is by faith and trust, not by works or legalism. The objector might ask, What if the Jews have never heard of Jesus Christ? How could they believe or call on Him? One cannot hear unless someone proclaims the good news. The only way for someone to declare His name is for God to send a preacher. Paul quotes Isaiah 52:7, where people welcome someone who brings good news. Paul reasoned that Isaiah said there were already messengers sent by God (15).

Another objection was that Israel did not obey the good news. Paul answered that Israel's rejection of Jesus was to be expected. Isaiah said long ago in despair, "Lord, who has believed our report?" (Isaiah 53:1, Romans 10:16 NKJV). The Jew's rejection of Jesus was a continuation of their pattern of disobeying God.

Again, the objector felt the Jews never had the opportunity to hear. In verse 18, Paul quotes Psalm 19:4 to show that the "line is gone out through all the earth, and their words to the end of the world." Paul points out God's message has gone out to all the world (Romans 1:18–23).

Another objection was that Israel might not understand. Paul responded that this question was absurd. The Jews were God's chosen people. They had every advantage. Israel may have failed to understand, but the Gentiles, who did not have all of the advantages of the Jews, did understand (19). To explain, Paul quoted Deuteronomy 32:21, where it states God would provoke the Jews to jealousy by a people who were not the chosen people.

Paul quoted another passage that stated God was found by people who were not looking for Him (Isaiah 65:1, Romans 10:20).

Paul closed his answer to the objector by pointing out that God has always reached out to Israel, but they were disobedient and contrary (Isaiah 65:2, Romans 10:21). God is not at fault. The Jews had a choice. Many refused God's offer of grace through faith in Jesus and chose the way of rules and traditions. Paul stressed that the Jews had personal responsibility for their choices. They had every opportunity to know the truth.

Everything begins and ends with God, but everything involves our human choices. God has given us free will, and we can accept or reject God's offer of salvation. It may be hard to grasp, but God is in control and has given us the freedom to choose. Paul sought to explain people's sins and God's plan of salvation. From God's perspective, He offers grace. From our perspective, we respond in faith.

Paul gave this testimony: "I have fought the good fight, I have finished the race, I have kept the faith" (2 Timothy 4:7 NKJV). Will we be able to give this same testimony one day? Paul wrote to Timothy, "Fight the good fight of faith, lay hold of eternal life, to which you were called and have confessed the good confession in the presence of many witnesses" (1 Timothy 6:12 NKJV).

CHAPTER 11

THE REMNANT

Paul continued to deal with the problem that the people God called to follow Him, obey Him, and witness to the world had rejected the Lord Jesus Christ.

GOD AND THE JEWS

I say then, Hath God cast away his people? God forbid. For I also am an Israelite, of the seed of Abraham, of the tribe of Benjamin. God hath not cast away his people which he foreknew. Wot ye not what the scripture saith of Elias? how he maketh intercession to God against Israel saying, Lord, they have killed thy prophets, and digged down thine altars; and I am left alone, and they seek my life. But what saith the answer of God unto him? I have reserved to myself seven thousand men, who have not bowed the knee to the image of Baal. Even so then at this present time also there is a remnant according to the election of grace. And if by grace, then is it no more of works: otherwise grace is no more grace. But if it be of works, then it is no more grace: otherwise work is no more work (Romans 11:1–6).

The question was if God had rejected Israel. Paul again responded with the strongest "No" in the Greek language. After all, Paul was an Israelite, of the seed of Abraham of the tribe of Benjamin" (1). Paul then used the experience of Elijah after the victory on Mount Carmel as an illustration. Later, Elijah was in despair because he thought he was the only faithful person left. But God told him seven thousand had not bowed to Baal (2–4). Paul concluded that a remnant of the faithful remained in Israel because of God's grace (5). God has chosen to offer grace to all sinners who respond to Him in faith.

The idea of the remnant developed in Israel after Elijah's experience. For example, Amos 9:8–10 pictures God sifting people in a sieve as we do flour until only the good remains. Micah had a vision of God gathering the faithful remnant of Israel (Micah 2:12, 5:3; see also Zephaniah 3:12–13). Jeremiah prophesied that a remnant would be gathered from the nations where the Jews had been scattered (Jeremiah 3:23). Ezekiel said that people were saved, not by being Jews, but by their own righteousness (Ezekiel 14:14, 20, 22). Isaiah named his son Shear-Jashub, which meant "salvation of the remnant" or "A remnant shall return" (Isaiah 7:3).

Salvation is an individual matter. No group or people are saved in total. Each person must have a personal relationship with the Lord. Each person must follow and trust Jesus as Lord for themselves.

People are not saved by their national citizenship, church membership, or family relationship. We do not inherit salvation. A person is saved when they respond to the grace of God through faith (6).

ISRAEL'S PATTERN OF REBELLION

What then? Israel hath not obtained that which he seeketh for; but the election hath obtained it, and the rest were blinded. (According as it is written, God hath given them the spirit of slumber, eyes that they should not see, and ears that they should not hear;) unto this day. And David saith, Let their table be made a snare, and a trap, and a stumblingblock, and a recompence unto them: Let their eyes be darkened, that they may not see, and bow down their back alway (Romans 11:7–10).

Paul argues that the nation as a whole has not been rejected. Those who were saved were saved by grace, not works. The Jews sought to be saved by works, but that wouldn't work. They had to be saved by grace through faith because faith works. Verse 7 says the rest were blinded. The Greek word is our word "callus." In Paul's day, it was used for the callus, which forms around a broken bone, which helps it heal and become even stronger. Paul said a callus had grown over the hearts of the people. The people had refused to see, hear, and obey the Lord. If we go our way long enough, we may reach the point where we no longer hear or see the Lord at work. Just as a callus can grow on our hands, a callus can also grow on our hearts.

Paul then quotes two Old Testament passages (Deuteronomy 29:4, Isaiah 29:10) to show that the people had continued to rebel so that they could not see or hear from God. God confirmed their decision to reject Him. They refused to see or perceive who God was or what He was doing, which resulted in spiritual blindness (8).

Paul also quotes what David wrote in Psalm 69:22–23: "Let this table become a snare." The picture shows the Jews sitting at a banquet table, feasting comfortably. They were at ease in Zion (Amos 6:1). They were so secure in their belief that being descendants of Abraham was all that was necessary for their salvation that this idea blinded them to the truth. Salvation was by grace through faith in the Lord Jesus Christ. Yet, the Jews, for the most part, rejected Jesus.

ISRAEL'S TOTAL REJECTION

I say then, Have they stumbled that they should fall? God forbid: but rather through their fall salvation is come unto the Gentiles, for to provoke them to jealousy. Now if the fall of them be the riches of the world, and the diminishing of them the riches of the Gentiles; how much more their fulness? For I speak to you Gentiles, inasmuch as I am the apostle of the Gentiles, I magnify mine office: If by any means I may provoke to emulation them which are my flesh, and might save some of them. For if the casting away of them be the reconciling of the world, what shall the receiving of them be, but life from the dead? (Romans 11:11–15).

Out of the failure of most of the Jews to receive Jesus, God brought something good. Their rejection opened the door of salvation to the Gentiles (11). The hope of salvation was extended to those who would respond in faith and receive Jesus as Savior and Lord. Paul still had the hope that the Jews would respond one day. Because of the fall of the Jews, the Gentiles came in by faith. But how much more complete it will be when the Jews are gathered in (12).

Paul then turns his attention to the Gentiles. Jesus called Paul to be an apostle to the Gentiles (13). This was Paul's main ministry, yet he still hoped the Jews would receive Jesus as their Lord and Savior (14). If they accepted Jesus, the change would be as radical as life from the dead (15).

GENTILES GRAFTED IN

For if the firstfruit be holy, the lump is also holy: and if the root be holy, so are the branches. And if some of the branches be broken off, and thou, being a wild olive tree, wert grafted in among them, and with them partakest of the root and fatness of the olive tree; Boast not against the branches. But if thou boast, thou bearest not the root, but the root thee (Romans 11:16–18).

Paul uses illustrations to explain the situation of the Jews and the Gentiles concerning their position with the Lord. The first illustration was the tradition of dedicating the first lump of dough to the Lord. This made all the rest of the dough holy (16, see Numbers 15:19–20). The offering of the first part to the Lord sanctified the whole. The other illustration entailed a tree. When planted, it was dedicated to the Lord. The resulting growth of the branches would be included (16).

Abraham and the other patriarchs of Israel were faithful to the Lord so that the resulting nation would be special to God. The present Jews learned about the faith handed down from their believing ancestors. Today, none of us stand alone in the faith. We stand on the faithfulness and testimony of believers who have gone before us. These believers include pastors, Bible teachers, family members, and friends who have shared their testimonies of faith and encouraged us to follow Jesus.

The statement about roots and branches (16) led Paul to continue with an illustration of the olive tree (17) — the most common and valuable tree in their world. The prophets said that the nation of Israel was God's olive tree (Jeremiah 11:16, Hosea 14:6).

Paul compares the Gentiles to branches of a wild olive tree grafted into a garden olive tree, which was Israel. The Gentiles had been on the outside, but by God's grace, they were brought into the root and fatness of the olive tree (17).

Paul then warns the Gentiles. They should not boast about their new position with God. The root supported the Gentiles. Christianity emerged from God's plan of the ages, working with and through the Jews (18).

GENTILES GRAFTED IN BY FAITH

Thou wilt say then, The branches were broken off, that I might be grafted in. Well; because of unbelief they were broken off, and thou standest by faith. Be not highminded, but fear: For if God spared not the natural branches, take heed lest he also spare not thee. Behold therefore the goodness and severity of God: on them which fell, severity; but toward thee, goodness, if thou continue in his goodness: otherwise thou also shalt be cut off. And they also, if they abide not still in unbelief, shall be grafted in: for God is able to graft them in again (Romans 11:19–23).

The Gentiles might be tempted to boast because the Jews were broken off, and they were grafted in (19). But the church has a debt to the faithful Jews who, through the centuries, helped prepare the way for the coming of the Messiah, the Lord Jesus Christ.

The Jews were broken off because of unbelief. The Gentiles were grafted in because of their faith. But the Gentiles should not be haughty about it because God's plan of grace was to bring salvation to all who believe (20). This is a warning of judgment. If God judged the natural branches, He would judge the arrogant, prideful branches who feel they deserve God's grace (21). Paul wanted the Gentiles to realize both the love ("goodness") and justice ("severity") of God. The challenge for the Gentiles was to continue in God's goodness instead of becoming filled with pride.

JEWS GRAFTED IN AGAIN BY FAITH

And they also, if they abide not still in unbelief, shall be grafted in: for God is able to graft them in again. For if thou wert cut out of the olive tree which is wild by nature, and wert grafted contrary to nature into a good olive tree: how much more shall these, which be the natural branches, be grafted into their own olive tree? For I would not, brethren, that ye should be ignorant of this mystery, lest ye should be wise in your own conceits; that blindness in part is happened to Israel, until the fulness of the Gentiles be come in. And so all Israel shall be saved: as it is written, There shall come out of Sion the Deliverer, and shall turn away ungodliness from Jacob: For this is my covenant unto them, when I shall take away their sins (Romans 11:23–27).

Paul had hoped that if the Jews would turn from their unbelief and believe in Jesus, they would be grafted back into the olive tree. "God is able!" Paul said. This is one of the most outstanding characteristics of the Lord. The phrase occurs many times in the Bible. Yes, our God can do whatever He wants.

Since the Gentiles were the wild olive tree and unnaturally grafted into the garden olive tree, it would be possible for the natural branches to be grafted back into the garden olive tree (24).

Paul revealed to the Gentiles a mystery that had been unknown. God used the rejection of most of the Jews to send the gospel to the Gentiles (25).

As Paul neared the end of his argument, he searched for why God's chosen people had rejected God's own Son. Paul knew the Jews had personal responsibility for their failure to believe in Jesus. He believed that God was in control but that the Jews were responsible for their actions. Paul also believed that the Jewish rejection of Jesus did not involve all Jews and was not permanent. He hoped the Jews would be saved (26). He quoted Isaiah 59:20–21 as hope for a time when the covenant would stand, and God would take away their sin (26–27).

ENEMIES OF GOD

As concerning the gospel, they are enemies for your sakes: but as touching the election, they are beloved for the father's sakes. For the gifts and calling of God are without repentance. For as ye in times past have not believed God, yet have now obtained mercy through their unbelief: Even so have these also now not believed, that through your mercy they also may obtain mercy (Romans 11:28–31).

The Jews had become God's enemies because they refused the gracious gift of God: salvation through Jesus (28). Now, they were under God's judgment. Yet, God had chosen them for a purpose, and they had a special place in God's plan (29). Paul believed in the end, the Jews would respond.

The Gentiles were once disobedient, but they had received the gospel when the Jews disobeyed (30). So now, even though the Jews are disobedient, they may respond to God's mercy since they have seen the mercy granted to the Gentiles (31).

A HYMN OF PRAISE

For God hath concluded them all in unbelief, that he might have mercy upon all. O the depth of the riches both of the wisdom and knowledge of God! how unsearchable are his judgments, and his ways past finding out! For who hath known the mind of the Lord? or who hath been his counsellor?

Or who hath first given to him, and it shall be recompensed unto him again? For of him, and through him, and to him, are all things: to whom be glory for ever. Amen (Romans 11:32–36).

Paul closed this section with a beautiful hymn of praise. No comments are necessary. Read it slowly and prayerfully in honor and praise to the Lord.

CHAPTER 12

LIVING FOR CHRIST

In this chapter, Paul turns to practical problems that believers confront. Usually, in Paul's letters, he first dealt with spiritual problems he knew were or might affect the church. Then, he would deal with practical issues about how a person should live daily for Christ.

TRUE WORSHIP AND RADICAL CHANGE

I beseech you therefore, brethren, by the mercies of God, that ye present your bodies a living sacrifice, holy, acceptable unto God, which is your reasonable service. And be not conformed to this world: but be ye transformed by the renewing of your mind, that ye may prove what is that good, and acceptable, and perfect, will of God. For I say, through the grace given unto me, to every man that is among you, not to think of himself more highly than he ought to think; but to think soberly, according as God hath dealt to every man the measure of faith (Romans 12:1-3).

Paul challenges the Christians in Rome to present their bodies to God. Our bodies belong to God as much as our spirits. We are to serve the Lord with our total self. Our body is the temple of the Holy Spirit who dwells in us (1 Corinthians 6:19). God sent His Son to take on human flesh and to live and work in a human body (John 1:1, 14).

Everything we do daily can be an offering and act of worship to God. The phrase, reasonable service, means worshipworthy of the Lord. We often use the phrase, worship service. Initially, the word in Greek for "service" was "to work for someone for pay." Finally, the word came to mean "service to the gods." In the Bible, the word is always used for service or worship to God. We don't just worship God in church. Wherever we are, we should be aware of His presence and offer ourselves to Him in reverence and awe (1).

To live this way requires a radical change. We should not be conformed to this world but be transformed. Conformed and transformed are difficult words to translate. Conform means to form or mold. Paul challenged believers not to allow the world around them to mold them into its image. Believers are not to accept the values, morals, or fads of society. Instead, we must be transformed by renewing our minds. "Transform" translates the Greek word from which we derive the word "metamorphosis," the word used for the dramatic change that happens to a caterpillar in a cocoon when it emerges as a butterfly. When we dedicate our minds to God's truth and let His Holy Spirit lead us, we will focus on God's good and acceptable and perfect will (2).

Another result of our lives given to God as a living sacrifice is that we will think clearly or soberly about who we are. Paul had accomplished this through the grace of God. We can avoid boasting and humble ourselves before God by faith and trust in God (3). We realize that we are His servants and servants in His church.

SPIRITUAL GIFTS

For as we have many members in one body, and all members have not the same office: So we, being many, are one body in Christ, and every one members one of another. Having then gifts differing according to the grace that is given to us, whether prophecy, let us prophesy according to the proportion of faith; Or ministry, let us wait on our ministering: or he that teacheth, on teaching; Or he that exhorteth, on exhortation: he that giveth, let him do it with simplicity; he that ruleth, with diligence; he that sheweth mercy, with cheerfulness (Romans 12:4–8).

Paul reminded the Roman church that God distributes the gifts (3).

He illustrated this using the human body. There are many different parts in the body, but they must work together despite having different functions (4). Paul pointed out that the church has many members, but they are one body in Christ and dependent on one another. The church is a unified body under the lordship of Jesus Christ (5).

Paul notes that every Christian has a God-given gift to be used in the church to reach a lost world (6). The Greek word for "gift" refers to God-given abilities to be used for His purposes and glory.

The first gift Paul lists is prophecy. Prophecy is not always future-telling but most often forth-telling. Prophecy is proclaiming or revealing God's will and purpose for people in general and particular situations. It is used for preaching or speaking God's Word (6, see also Acts 13:1–3).

Ministry means service in contrast to the speaking gift (1 Peter 4:11). Our English word "deacon" is derived from the Greek word *diakonos*. Deacons and all believers can demonstrate the love of Christ in everyday acts of service for the Lord and others (7).

Another gift is teaching. The gospel must be proclaimed and explained (7). Over the years, when witnessing to adults in their homes, some have told me that no one had ever personally explained God's plan of salvation to them.

The next gift is exhortation. Believers should encourage one another. To exhort is the effort to motivate a person to continue his walk with the Lord (8).

The gift of giving must be done with liberality. This word carries the meaning of simplicity and generosity. Christian giving should be in simple kindness, just for the joy of giving. Believers are to be givers, not takers (8).

Some are gifted with leadership. Every church needs people gifted by God to lead in the church's various ministries. Whether in a small or a prominent role, a person should use the gift of leadership with diligence or zeal. The church also needs people who will lead with enthusiasm (8).

The last gift Paul mentions is showing mercy. When we forgive, we should not do it begrudgingly. An old saying says, "I forgive you, but I won't forget." We must forgive, forget, and let go of wrongs done to us. We must forgive with cheerfulness (8).

BEHAVE LIKE A CHRISTIAN

Let love be without dissimulation. Abhor that which is evil; cleave to that which is good. Be kindly affectioned one to another with brotherly love; in honour preferring one another; not slothful in business; fervent in spirit; serving the Lord; rejoicing in hope; patient in tribulation; continuing instant in prayer; distributing to the necessity of saints; given to hospitality (Romans 12:9–13).

Paul lists important points of the believers' everyday life in Christ, like writing a sermon outline.

Love must be completely sincere. There should be no pretending, play-acting, or other agenda. We should care for others lovingly (9).

Hate what is evil. We are to abhor or hate what is evil but cling to what is good. These are strong words. The one place for hate is to hate evil. Good is not just something to think about but something to wrap our arms around and hang onto (9).

Love one another. There are three Greek words to express love in verses 9 and 10. The word *agape* is used first. This word describes God's kind of love that always puts others first. The next word for love is *philo*, which means brotherly love (hence, Philadelphia, the city of brotherly love). The last word, *philostorgos* means family love and is translated here as kindly affectionate. We are all members of the same family, the family of God. As Christians, we are brothers and sisters and have one Father, Almighty God.

In honor, prefer one another. Many problems happen in churches when someone wants the spotlight. Some people desire places of privilege, power, or praise. We should be humble and put others before ourselves (10).

Don't be lazy. Paul wrote, "not lagging in diligence." Life is short, and opportunities to serve the Lord and His kingdom are now. Have a zeal and a sense of urgency in your walk with the Lord (11).

Be fervent in spirit. Jesus rebuked the church at Laodicea because it was neither cold nor hot (Revelation 3:15–16). We should be a flame, shining in a dark world. Our hearts should be on fire for Jesus (11).

Serve the Lord. The main goal of all these admonitions is to focus on our service to the Lord. We are not just serving people, the church, or the community. Instead, we are serving the Lord (11).

Rejoice in hope. There is no such thing as a hopeless Christian. Above all others on earth, the Christian has hope. Our hope is based on our relationship with our Savior, the Lord Jesus Christ. His grace is sufficient in all situations (2 Corinthians 12:9). He works through all things for our good according to His will in Christ Jesus (12, see also Romans 8:28).

Be patient in tribulation. We can persevere through the most challenging times because of the presence of the Lord. Before the three Hebrew boys — Shadrach, Meshach, and Abednego — were thrown into the fiery furnace, they declared, "Our God whom we serve is able to deliver us. … But if not … we do not serve your gods, nor will we worship the gold image which you have set up" (Daniel 3:17–18 NKJV). We can face anything when we face it with Jesus Christ (12).

Continue in prayer. In 1 Thessalonians 5:17, Paul challenged the church to "pray without ceasing." Being in the attitude of prayer continually is essential to remain close to the will and purpose of the Lord for our lives. If we disconnect, we rob ourselves of the Lord's wisdom, power, and strength (12).

Help with the physical needs of the saints. A believer should major in giving rather than receiving. In Paul's day, many believers were disowned by their families, excluded from society, and faced with losing their jobs. It was important to help one another (13).

Be hospitable. This word means "love of strangers." There were many traveling Christians and missionaries but few decent inns or places to stay when traveling. Christians depended upon the love and hospitality of fellow believers. Believers were to have an open door and open hand attitude, especially to other believers (Hebrews 12:12, 1 Timothy 3:2, Titus 1:8, and 1 Peter 4:9).

BEHAVE LIKE A CHRISTIAN TO OUTSIDERS

Bless them which persecute you: bless, and curse not. Rejoice with them that do rejoice, and weep with them that weep. Be of the same mind one toward another. Mind not high things, but condescend to men of low estate. Be not wise in your own conceits. Recompense to no man evil for evil. Provide things honest in the sight of all men. If it be possible, as much as lieth in you, live peaceably with all men. Dearly beloved, avenge not yourselves, but rather give place unto wrath: for it is written, Vengeance is mine; I will repay, saith the Lord. Therefore if thine enemy hunger, feed him; if he thirst, give him drink: for in so doing thou shalt heap coals of fire on his head. Be not overcome of evil, but overcome evil with good (Romans 12:14–21).

Paul also instructed believers on how to relate to others outside the church.

Bless, don't curse. A believer must meet persecution with a prayer for those persecuting them. Bless means to speak well of or to praise. When we are insulted or mistreated because of our faith, we are not to seek revenge but to pray for our persecutor (14). When Jesus hung on the cross, He prayed for forgiveness for those who put Him there (Luke 23:34).

Rejoice and weep. These two things, taken together, can create a bond between people as they go through life's changing circumstances, when they are happy or sad. To rejoice with someone else when they succeed or pass through times of sorrow can strengthen a relationship (15).

Be like-minded. For a church to function as the body of Christ, all the parts must work together in harmony. We may not always agree on everything, but we should agree about our faith, the gospel, our purpose, our mission, and our loyalty to the Lord Jesus Christ (16).

Be humble. We should avoid pride and the better-than-you attitude. Our standing with Christ has nothing to do with our social standing, wealth, or family background. God does not play favorites, and neither should we. We should treat all people with kindness and the love of Christ and not place ourselves above them (16).

Live peacefully. We are to seek to live in peace and be peacemakers (Matthew 5:9). We are not to return evil for evil but, as much as possible, live peacefully with all people (18). We should have regard for the good. Good means morally good (17). This doesn't mean we tolerate evil or close our eyes to those doing it. There will be a time when we must take our stand with Jesus, no matter how difficult that may be (17–18).

Do not avenge. We should not seek personal revenge but allow God to be the judge. Vengeance belongs to the Lord, not us. We are not fit to judge one another. Paul quoted Proverbs 25:21–23 to explain that we should show mercy even to our enemies. The way to overcome evil is with good (21). The expression, heap coals of fire, means this might bring them shame and repentance. We might then have a friend rather than an enemy.

Paul rapidly laid out many points of emphasis that should characterize our daily lives. He revealed that the Lord's will concerns our salvation and how we live concerning Him and others.

CHAPTER 13

THE CHRISTIAN AND THE STATE

Paul seems to suddenly change his focus by pointing out the Christians' obligation to the government. Paul wrote about this in his letters to Timothy and Titus (1 Timothy 2:1-2; Titus 3:1). Peter also wrote, "Submit yourselves to every ordinance of man for the Lord's sake ... for this is the will of God, that by doing good you may put to silence the ignorance of foolish men ... Honor all people. Love the brotherhood. Fear God. Honor the king" (1 Peter 2:13–17 NKJV).

CHRISTIAN DUTY

Let every soul be subject unto the higher powers. For there is no power but of God: the powers that be are ordained of God. Whosoever therefore resisteth the power, resisteth the ordinance of God: and they that resist shall receive to themselves damnation. For rulers are not a terror to good works, but to the evil. Wilt thou then not be afraid of the power? do that which is good, and thou shalt have praise of the same: For he is the minister of God to thee for good. But if thou do that which is evil, be afraid; for he beareth not the sword in vain: for he is the minister of God, a revenger to execute wrath upon him that doeth evil. Wherefore ye must needs be subject, not only for wrath, but also for conscience sake (Romans 13:1-5).

God's plan was for believers to respect the governing authorities, even if it was the evil Nero. Nero ruled the Roman Empire from AD 54–68 and persecuted Christians. Paul wrote to the Romans while Nero was in power.

Believers are not to resist governmental authority because this will bring their judgment. Paul is not speaking about eternal punishment. But God can use human punishment to curb criminal behavior (2).

Why would Paul write these instructions? Most people are not hermits but are involved in society and live in a country. We should live in a non-criminal manner so that others will realize that Christians are not troublemakers or threats to society. The Jewish Zealots were known for their terrorist activities and attempts to overthrow the government. The Lord wants us to be identified as His followers, not proponents of chaos, discord, and rebellion (3).

But, as Paul saw it, the Roman Empire was being used by God to bring peace and order in Paul's day. Roman peace made travel and mail service convenient and brought many other benefits to society (4).

The authorities were in place to execute wrath on evildoers. The sword was a means of execution. Beheading was the most common method of capital punishment (4).

The phrase "for conscience's sake" in verse 5 refers to believers being subject to the government because of their civic duty. But it is also a believer's spiritual duty to God.

PUBLIC DEBT

For for this cause pay ye tribute also: for they are God's ministers, attending continually upon this very thing. Render therefore to all their dues: tribute to whom tribute is due; custom to whom custom; fear to whom fear; honour to whom honour (Romans 13:6–7).

Verses 6 and 7 have two types of public debts. Taxes were paid by those who lived in a nation under the control of Rome. But there were other taxes as well. A farmer had to pay one-tenth of his grain crop and one-fifth of the wine and fruit he produced. There was also an income tax of 1 percent of income. Additionally, everyone between the ages of fourteen and sixty-five had to pay a poll tax (6).

There were also customs taxes, including import and export taxes and taxes for using roads, bridges, markets, and harbors. Taxes were also assessed for the animals a person owned and any cart or wagon they had (7).

Paul encouraged believers to pay these public debts no matter how difficult. Jesus said, "Render therefore to Caesar the things that are Caesar's, and to God the things that are God's" (Matthew 22:21 NKJV).

DEALING WITH DEBTS

Owe no man any thing, but to love one another: for he that loveth another hath fulfilled the law. For this, Thou shalt not commit adultery, Thou shalt not kill, Thou shalt not steal, Thou shalt not bear false witness, Thou shalt not covet; and if there be any other commandment, it is briefly comprehended in this saying, namely, Thou shalt love thy neighbour as thyself. Love worketh no ill to his neighbour: therefore love is the fulfilling of the law (Romans 13:8–10).

Being a Christian does not exempt us from acting responsibly with our financial obligations. When we don't pay our debts, it reflects poorly on other believers and our Lord (8).

There is a debt we can never pay off: our debt to love others (8). But when we seek to pay this debt of love, we fulfill the commandments (9). Paul listed some commandments that deal with our relationship with others: do not commit adultery, kill, steal, or covet. These commandments can be summed up in one command: "Thou shalt love thy neighbour as thyself" (9). Love does not harm others and completely fulfills the law (10).

THE PROBLEM OF TIME

And that, knowing the time, that now it is high time to awake out of sleep: for now is our salvation nearer than when we believed. The night is far spent, the day is at hand: let us therefore cast off the works of darkness, and let us put on the armour of light. Let us walk honestly, as in the day; not in rioting and drunkenness, not in chambering and wantonness, not in strife and envying. But put ye on the Lord Jesus Christ, and make not provision for the flesh, to fulfil the lusts thereof (Romans 13:11–14).

We must be aware of the time because we live in the last days. The next event in Biblical prophecy is the return of the Lord Jesus for His church. We must be alert and ready for His return. Our salvation is nearer means that the consummation of our salvation is near. This refers to the return of Christ (11).

"Night" is the present time when Satan is still at work. "The day" is a common expression in the Bible for the day of the Lord — when the Lord will establish His eternal reign, and judgment will occur (12).

We are to cast off the works of disobedience and put on the armor of light. Paul wrote about a more complete picture of the Christians' armor in Ephesians 6:10–17. The Christian armor includes a truth-girded waist, a breastplate of righteousness, gospel-shodded feet, a shield of faith, a helmet of salvation, and a sword of the Spirit. We are to live as children of the light, not in riotous behavior, drunkenness, or lewd or lustful living. Paul included strife and envy with these evil attitudes and actions (13). Causing strife and being envious of others is all too common, even in churches. These attitudes and actions can cause as much havoc as drunkenness and lustful behavior.

On a positive note, Paul said since believers have cast off evil things, they should put on the Lord Jesus Christ. We should not let the lust of our human nature rule over us (14). To put on Christ means that believers should imitate the characteristics of our Lord. Paul described these characteristics in Galatians 5:22–23: "But the fruit of the Spirit is love, joy, peace, long-suffering, kindness, goodness, faithfulness, gentleness, self-control" (NKJV).

CHAPTER 14

THE LAW OF LIBERTY AND THE LAW OF LOVE

Paul begins dealing with the problem of judging one another within the church. First, he deals with the issue of what is proper to eat and then with whether certain days are more special than others.

THE QUESTION OF FOOD

Him that is weak in the faith receive ye, but not to doubtful disputations. For one believeth that he may eat all things: another, who is weak, eateth herbs. Let not him that eateth despise him that eateth not; and let not him which eateth not judge him that eateth: for God hath received him. Who art thou that judgest another man's servant? To his own master he standeth or falleth. Yea, he shall be holden up: for God is able to make him stand (Romans 14:1–4).

The Jews, as well as many other nations, observed certain food laws. The book of Leviticus lists many excluded foods. Even today, some foods are considered kosher by the Jews, and some are not. Paul felt that a mature believer should know that anything God made was not common or unclean. In Acts 10:10–16, Peter's vision settled that issue for many Christians. At the close of the vision, a voice declared to Peter, "What God has cleansed you must not call common" (NKJV).

Paul wanted the church to accept the weaker person in the faith (1). The weaker person was the one who kept the strict food rules. Paul did not want food to be an issue that would divide the fellowship (2). He pleaded with both sides of the food issue. The one who sees no wrong in eating meat should not despise the one who won't eat meat. And the one who won't eat meat should not judge those who do (3).

Paul used the illustration of a servant. A servant was only accountable to his master. No one had the right to judge or criticize another person's servant. All believers are servants of Christ. So, Paul concluded, "God is able to make him stand" (4). God is the Judge, and He receives believers, whether babies in Christ or mature believers.

The weak in the faith still had faith. Although they trusted Jesus as Lord and Savior, they had not matured in the faith as much as others. They still clung to the old food laws. Paul taught that food was clean if they had thanked God (1 Timothy 4:3–5).

THE QUESTION OF HOLY DAYS

One man esteemeth one day above another: another esteemeth every day alike. Let every man be fully persuaded in his own mind. He that regardeth the day, regardeth it unto the Lord; and he that regardeth not the day, to the Lord he doth not regard it. He that eateth, eateth to the Lord, for he giveth God thanks; and he that eateth not, to the Lord he eateth not, and giveth God thanks (Romans 14:5–6).

One day above another probably referred to the many holy days in the Jewish calendar. Some wanted to continue all the holy day observances, and others thought all days were alike. People had strong convictions on both sides of this issue, but each had the right to his convictions (5).

Both groups should honor the Lord, whether they keep a particular day or not. This applied also to the food issue. Both groups should thank the Lord whether they ate vegetables or meat (6).

PROPER PERSPECTIVE

For none of us liveth to himself, and no man dieth to himself. For whether we live, we live unto the Lord; and whether we die, we die unto the Lord: whether we live therefore, or die, we are the Lord's. For to this end Christ both died, and rose, and revived, that he might be Lord both of the dead and living. But why dost thou judge thy brother? Or why dost thou set at nought thy brother? for we shall all stand before the judgment seat of Christ. For it is written, As I live, saith the Lord, every knee shall bow to me, and every tongue shall confess to God. So then every one of us shall give account of himself to God. Let us not therefore judge one another any more: but judge this rather, that no man put a stumblingblock or an occasion to fall in his brother's way (Romans 14:7–13).

None of us refers to believers. There is no such thing as a Lone Ranger Christian. Because of our union with Christ, we are united with one another. Our goal should be to worship and serve the Lord together (7).

For a believer, all our life is lived with Christ. The Holy Spirit dwells in us, so whether we are alive or dead, we are with the Lord (8). This unity with Christ was why Jesus went to the cross to die for our sins. He rose again and lived so that "he might be Lord both of the dead and living" (9).

Since Jesus is Lord and we are one family in Him, Paul asks another question, "Why dost thou judge thy brother? Or why dost thou set at nought [show contempt for] thy brother?" (10). Paul was addressing weak and strong believers. The weak were not to judge, and the strong were not to show contempt. The word "contempt" is the same word translated as "despise" in verse 3. We are not to judge because we will all stand before the judgment seat of Christ (10).

Paul quoted Isaiah 45:23 to show that one day, everyone will have to submit to God's authority, and He will judge all people (11). We will all give an account to God about our behavior (12).

Paul concluded that we should not judge one another since God was the Judge. We should be determined to do everything possible to keep from harming our brothers and sisters in Christ (13).

THE LAW OF LOVE

I know, and am persuaded by the Lord Jesus, that there is nothing unclean of itself: but to him that esteemeth any thing to be unclean, to him it is unclean. But if thy brother be grieved with thy meat, now walkest thou not charitably. Destroy not him with thy meat, for whom Christ died. Let not then your good be evil spoken of: For the kingdom of God is not meat and drink; but righteousness, and peace, and joy in the Holy Ghost. For he that in these things serveth Christ is acceptable to God, and approved of men (Romans 14:14–18).

The Lord Jesus convinced Paul that all food was clean. But if a person felt it was wrong to eat certain food, it was unclean for him. Unclean meant common and referred to the Jewish ceremonial food laws (14). If a believer, who sees no wrong in eating certain foods, hurts a fellow believer by doing so, he is not living a loving Christian lifestyle (15).

Love is the law that should rule our hearts. Our liberty to eat what we want might destroy the weak one. So, the rule of love would dictate that we do not eat meat if it harms a weaker believer for whom Christ died (15). Believers are not to use their freedom to be spoken of as evil. What we consider good might be considered evil by others (16).

We may enjoy hobbies, pastimes, or customs, but they are not essential to the Christian life. These things we should change if they offend a weaker brother. We should be aware of how our actions affect others. But we cannot let the opinions of other people dominate our lives. Our conduct should be guided by the principle of God's love, righteousness, peace, and joy in the Holy Spirit (17). If we major on these three godly characteristics, our conduct will be acceptable to God and approved by others (18).

PURSUE PEACE

Let us therefore follow after the things which make for peace, and things wherewith one may edify another. For meat destroy not the work of God. All things indeed are pure; but it is evil for that man who eateth with offence. It is good neither to eat flesh, nor to drink wine, nor any thing whereby thy brother stumbleth, or is offended, or is made weak. Hast thou faith? have it to thyself before God. Happy is he that condemneth not himself in that thing which he alloweth. And he that doubteth is damned if he eat, because he eateth not of faith: for whatsoever is not of faith is sin (Romans 14:19–23).

Paul concludes this section with some challenges for believers. Christian freedom is not the freedom to harm another person spiritually, mentally, or physically. Paul set before the believers in Rome two great goals.

One was to pursue things that made peace. Pursue means to work for peace actively. A church characterized by division, quarrels, and strife is not a part of the true church of the Lord Jesus. It is simply an earthly club with no heavenly purpose. The goal is for everyone to have a right relationship with the Lord and each other (19).

The second goal is for church members to edify one another. The word means to build up. Jesus is the foundation of the church, and we are like stones of the wall (1 Peter 2:4–8). Often, a church will stumble into controversy over little things that do not matter, like the color of the carpet or the color of the paint on the walls. We must take a stand when it is a question of biblical truth, the truth about the gospel, or the truth about God. But if a group does not consider one another in love, it is not a church of the Lord Jesus Christ (19).

We are not to destroy the fellowship of the church over food. All food is good, but it is evil if a person believes it to be evil for him (20). We are encouraged to avoid anything that will cause a fellow believer to stumble, be made weak, or be offended" (21). All three words describe the downfall of a fellow believer.

Paul also encouraged mature believers not to abandon their convictions about things not condemned by the law. They should have faith (22).

But if a weaker believer believes it is a sin to eat certain foods and does it, he is guilty of sin (23).

Our faith is the key to living our Christian lives in relationships with other believers. Paul asks, "Do you have faith?" (22 NKJV). If a person eats something against his conscience, he is not eating according to his faith (23). Whatever we do that is not guided by faith is a sin. This is a guiding principle for believers in matters of conduct. If any activity does not match up with New Testament faith in the Lord Jesus Christ, for a believer, it is a sin.

CHAPTER 15

WITH ONE MIND AND ONE VOICE

Paul continues his discussion about relating to a weaker brother that he began in the previous chapter.

BEAR ONE ANOTHER'S BURDENS

We then that are strong ought to bear the infirmities of the weak, and not to please ourselves. Let every one of us please his neighbour for his good to edification. For even Christ pleased not himself; but, as it is written, The reproaches of them that reproached thee fell on me. For whatsoever things were written aforetime were written for our learning, that we through patience and comfort of the scriptures might have hope. Now the God of patience and consolation grant you to be likeminded one toward another according to Christ Jesus: That ye may with one mind and one mouth glorify God, even the Father of our Lord Jesus Christ (Romans 15:1–6).

Strong believers should not try to please themselves but should bear or carry the load of the weaker person in Christ (1). The goal was that the strong should desire good for others, building them up in the faith (2).

Jesus is the prime example for a strong believer. Jesus did not seek to please Himself, but He took upon Himself the world's reproaches for all people so that all people would have a clear picture of God (3).

The Scriptures were written so we could learn more about the Lord and His plan for our lives. The Word of God enables us to endure and be encouraged, which results in hope. So, strong believers should be patient with the weak so that both of them will find hope in Christ (4).

Paul prayed for the church in Rome. He used the same two words that described the Scriptures to describe God. He prayed that the God of patience and comfort would enable the believers to be of one mind with each other (5). They were to have a mind toward each other as Christ Jesus had for them. Paul also prayed that they might be unified in their praise and worship of God, the Father of our Lord Jesus Christ (6).

GLORIFY GOD TOGETHER

Wherefore receive ye one another, as Christ also received us to the glory of God. Now I say that Jesus Christ was a minister of the circumcision for the truth of God, to confirm the promises made unto the fathers: And that the Gentiles might glorify God for his mercy; as it is written, For this cause I will confess to thee among the Gentiles, and sing unto thy name. And again he saith, Rejoice, ye Gentiles, with his people. And again, Praise the Lord, all ye Gentiles; and laud him, all ye people. And again, Esaias saith, There shall be a root of Jesse, and he that shall rise to reign over the Gentiles; in him shall the Gentiles trust. Now the God of hope fill you with all joy and peace in believing, that ye may abound in hope, through the power of the Holy Ghost (Romans 15:7–13).

With the standard being Christ Jesus, they were to accept each other as Christ had accepted them. This would bring glory to God (7). This verse introduced the conclusion of the discussion begun in chapter 14: "Receive one who is weak in the faith" (Romans 14:1 NKJV). The command to receive one another is not just for mature believers but for all believers.

Jesus became a servant to the Jews for three reasons: to fulfill the plan of God to bring salvation to the Jews and all people; to confirm the promises made to Abraham, Isaac, and Jacob; and to bring in the nations by the mercy of God so they could glorify and praise His name (8–9).

Paul then points to four Old Testament passages to prove it was

God's plan that both Jews and Gentiles glorify Him (9–12). Testimony and songs of praise would be proclaimed to the Gentiles (2 Samuel 22:50, Psalm 18:49). The Gentiles will be invited to rejoice with the people of God (Deuteronomy 31:43). All nations were called upon to praise the Lord (Psalm 117:1). The coming Messiah ("root of Jesse") will reign over the Gentiles, and in Him, the Gentiles shall hope (Isaiah 11:10).

Paul quoted from the Law, the Prophets, and the Psalms — the three divisions of the Scriptures according to the Jews. Paul quoted three great Old Testament leaders: Moses, David, and Isaiah. God's purpose was always for Israel to be His witness to the nations. Although Israel failed for the most part and failed to accept Jesus as the Messiah, there were both Jews and Gentiles in the churches.

Paul closed this section with a prayer that the God of hope would fill them abundantly ("full to overflowing") with hope. He also prayed that the church would be filled with joy and peace due to their faith. Hope, joy, and peace will come by the power of the Holy Spirit (13). Hope is not wishful thinking but confident expectation. God is the author of salvation and offers hope to all who respond to Him.

Called to Preach the Gospel

And I myself also am persuaded of you, my brethren, that ye also are full of goodness, filled with all knowledge, able also to admonish one another. Nevertheless, brethren, I have written the more boldly unto you in some sort, as putting you in mind, because of the grace that is given to me of God, that I should be the minister of Jesus Christ to the Gentiles, ministering the gospel of God, that the offering up of the Gentiles might be acceptable, being sanctified by the Holy Ghost (Romans 15:14–16).

Paul was confident that the believers in Rome would be faithful to the Lord. He described them as full of goodness and knowledge and able to encourage one another (14). Paul also gave them the reason he had spoken boldly to them. It reminded them of the truth of the practical aspects of the Christian life (15).

The reason for Paul's instruction was that God had called him to be a minister of the gospel to the Gentiles. The word ministering means priestly service. Paul pictured himself as a priest among the Gentiles, offering sacrifices to God. He offered to God Gentile believers who were made acceptable to God because they were sanctified or set apart by the Holy Spirit to serve God (16).

Personal Testimony

I have therefore whereof I may glory through Jesus Christ in those things which pertain to God. For I will not dare to speak of any of those things which Christ hath not wrought by me, to make the Gentiles obedient, by word and deed, through mighty signs and wonders, by the power of the Spirit of God; so that from Jerusalem, and round about unto Illyricum, I have fully preached the gospel of Christ. Yea, so have I strived to preach the gospel, not where Christ was named, lest I should build upon another man's foundation: But as it is written, To whom he was not spoken of, they shall see: and they that have not heard shall understand (Romans 15:17–21).

Paul concludes this section of his letter by making a point. He shared his testimony about how God had worked in the ministry God had called him to carry out. Paul had reason to boast about Christ Jesus because of all the things God had accomplished, but he declined to list them (17). Jesus Christ had used Paul in word and deed to challenge the Gentiles to be obedient (18).

The power of the Holy Spirit had done mighty signs and wonders, and Paul was enabled to preach the gospel from Jerusalem to Illyricum (19). Illyricum was north of Italy and Greece. Paul's goal was to be a pioneer missionary. He wanted to preach Christ where no one had gone before. He did not want to build on what others had started but to boldly go to those who had never heard the gospel. He quoted Isaiah 52:15 as the key verse for his missionary zeal (20–21).

PAUL'S PLAN TO VISIT ROME

For which cause also I have been much hindered from coming to you. But now having no more place in these parts, and having a great desire these many years to come unto you; whensoever I take my journey into Spain, I will come to you: for I trust to see you in my journey, and to be brought on my way thitherward by you, if first I be somewhat filled with your company (Romans 15:22–24).

For this reason refers to Paul's comments in verses 21–22. Since his goal was to preach Christ where Christ had never been preached, Paul had been too occupied to journey to Rome. Paul's plan had a long-range goal: to go on a missionary journey to Spain. He had covered the area between Jerusalem and Illyricum and desired to go to Spain. He also wanted to stop over with the believers in Rome on his way to Spain. He felt assured they would help him on his journey and looked forward to their fellowship (22–24).

PAUL'S MISSION TO JERUSALEM

But now I go unto Jerusalem to minister unto the saints. For it hath pleased them of Macedonia and Achaia to make a certain contribution for the poor saints which are at Jerusalem. It hath pleased them verily; and their debtors they are. For if the Gentiles have been made partakers of their spiritual things, their duty is also to minister unto them in carnal things. When therefore I have performed this, and have sealed to them this fruit, I will come by you into Spain (Romans 15:25–28).

Paul's plan also had a short-term goal. He had encouraged the Gentile churches that he had started to take an offering for the church in Jerusalem. The church members there were mainly Jews, and they were in difficult times. There was the Jewish persecution and loss of jobs for the believers. Paul believed the offering would help unify believers (25–27). After this important task had been accomplished, Paul planned to go to Spain (28).

PAUL ASKED FOR PRAYER

And I am sure that, when I come unto you, I shall come in the fulness of the blessing of the gospel of Christ. Now I beseech you, brethren, for the Lord Jesus Christ's sake, and for the love of the Spirit, that ye strive together with me in your prayers to God for me; that I may be delivered from them that do not believe in Judaea; and that my service which I have for Jerusalem may be accepted of the saints; that I may come unto you with joy by the will of God, and may with you be refreshed. Now the God of peace be with you all. Amen (Romans 15:29–33).

We don't know if Paul ever made it to Spain, but he did make it to Rome. It was not how he planned it, but the Lord had a special plan for Paul. Paul accomplished his mission to the church in Jerusalem but was attacked by the Jews and turned over to the Romans. Paul finally appealed to Caesar and was transferred to the court in Rome. Even as a prisoner, Paul testified about his faith in the emperor's court (Acts 25). He could also have visitors from the church. Paul was confident that when he arrived in Rome, he would impart the full blessing of the gospel of Christ (19).

Paul pleads with the believers in Rome that they would strive together with him in prayers for him. Strive carries the idea of working diligently or of running a race. It was not casual but the idea of earnest, consistent prayer. Paul sincerely wanted them to pray for him. He wanted this done through the Lord Jesus Christ and the love of the Spirit (30).

Paul gave three reasons why he coveted their prayers: he would be delivered from unbelieving Jews in Judea, the believers in Jerusalem would accept the love offering in the loving spirit in which it was given, and it would be the will of God that he could come to them with joy and they be renewed in the Lord. Paul closed this section with a brief prayer that the God of peace would be with them (31–32).

CHAPTER 16

ALL NATIONS OBEDIENT TO THE FAITH

Paul began his closing words to the church in Rome by commending Phoebe and greeting people in the church in Rome whom he knew personally. He also challenged them to avoid divisive persons. He then sent greetings from those who were serving the Lord with him.

COMMENDATION OF PHOEBE

I commend unto you Phebe [Phoebe] our sister, which is a servant of the church which is at Cenchrea: That ye receive her in the Lord, as becometh saints, and that ye assist her in whatsoever business she hath need of you: for she hath been a succourer of many, and of myself also (Romans 16:1–2).

Paul gave his words of recommendation for Phoebe, who was traveling to Rome. Some think she was the person who brought Paul's letter to Rome. She was commended as a sister in the faith and a servant of the church. This implied that she had some official position in the church. Phoebe came from Cenchrea, the port of Corinth (1).

Paul encouraged them to receive her in the Lord and assist her in any way possible. He told them she had helped many, including him. Helper means benefactor. Perhaps she was wealthy and had helped the church and Paul financially (2).

GREETING ROMAN CHRISTIANS

Greet Priscilla and Aquila my helpers in Christ Jesus: Who have for my life laid down their own necks: unto whom not only I give thanks, but also all the churches of the Gentiles. Likewise greet the church that is in their house. Salute my well-beloved Epaenetus, who is the firstfruits of Achaia unto Christ (Romans 16:3–5a).

This is the longest list of greetings in any of Paul's letters. He mentions twenty-six people — one-third of whom are women.

Priscilla and Aquila worked in the same trade (tent-making) as Paul. They worked with Paul in Corinth and Ephesus (3, see also Acts 18:1–3, 18, 26). This married couple is always listed together. The New Testament does not record how they risked their necks for Paul, but it may have happened in Ephesus. Paul and all the Gentile churches were grateful to them (4).

There was a church meeting in their home (5). First Corinthians 16:19 also mentions they had a church meeting in their home.

From Acts 18:2, we learn they were residents of Rome before meeting Paul. Emperor Claudius issued an order in AD 52 expelling Jews from Rome. When the ban was lifted, Priscilla, Aquila, and other Jews returned to Rome.

Every home ought to be a church where Jesus dwells and is honored and worshiped. We can use our homes and hospitality as witnessing aids to our lost friends.

A GREETING TO OTHERS

Likewise greet the church that is in their house. Salute my well-beloved Epaenetus, who is the firstfruits of Achaia unto Christ. Greet Mary, who bestowed much labour on us. Salute Andronicus and Junia, my kinsmen, and my fellow-prisoners, who are of note among the apostles, who also were in Christ before me. Greet Amplias my beloved in the Lord. Salute Urbane, our helper in Christ, and Stachys my beloved. Salute Apelles approved in Christ. Salute them which are of Aristobulus' household. Salute Herodion my kinsman. Greet them that be of the household of Narcissus, which are in the Lord. Salute Tryphena and Tryphosa, who labour in the Lord. Salute the beloved Persis, which laboured much in the Lord. Salute Rufus chosen in the Lord, and his mother and mine. Salute Asyncritus, Phlegon, Hermas, Patrobas, Hermes, and the brethren which are with them. Salute Philologus, and Julia, Nereus, and his sister, and Olympas, and all the saints which are with them. Salute one another with an holy kiss. The churches of Christ salute you (Romans 16:5b–16).

Of these twenty-four names, thirteen occur in inscriptions or documents related to the emperor's palace in Rome. Many of these are familiar names, but Paul spoke of believers in Caesar's household (Philippians 4:22). They could have been slaves or even extended members of the family of Caesar.

- Epaenetus was the first convert in Asia.
- Mary was a devoted worker in the church.
- Andronicus and Junias were kinsmen and fellow prisoners. They were early Christians and well-known among the apostles.
- Amplias was beloved in the Lord. This was a common slave name. In the early church, race, rank, and social standing distinctions were erased (8).
- Urbanus was a fellow worker in Christ. Stachys was beloved by the Lord (9).
- Apelles was approved by Christ. Several of these names were common slave names and have been found in lists of slaves who served in the emperor's household.
- Aristobulus was a familiar Greek name. The Herods used this name often. There was Aristobulus, who was a grandson of Herod the Great. Apparently, his whole family were believers (10).
- Herodian was a fellow countryman of Paul's.

- Narcissus' whole household was believers (11).
- Tryphena and Tryphosa labored in the Lord and were probably twins. These names mean dainty and delicate. Labor means to work to the point of exhaustion. Peris was a beloved worker, who also labored much in the Lord (12).
- Rufus was "chosen in the Lord, and his mother and mine." When Simon of Cyrene was compelled to carry the cross of Jesus, the Bible mentions that he was the father of Alexander and Rufus (Mark 15:21). They must have been well-known in the church for their names to be listed. They apparently became Christians and were active in the church. Rufus' mother must have been kind and supportive of Paul's ministry.
- Asyncritus, Phlegon, Hermas, Patrobus, and Hermes were further brethren. There were probably leaders of another house church. Paul also mentions Philologus, Julia, Nereus, and his sister Olympas as saints with them. This is yet another house church group, and the leaders were mentioned by name.

After sending greetings to believers he already knew, Paul encouraged the church to greet one another in Christian love with a holy kiss. A kiss on the cheek in the early church symbolized Christian love (1 Corinthians 16:20, 2 Corinthians 13:12; 1 Thessalonians 5:26; 1 Peter 5:14).

DIVISIVE PEOPLE

Now I beseech you, brethren, mark them which cause divisions and offences contrary to the doctrine which ye have learned; and avoid them. For they that are such serve not our Lord Jesus Christ, but their own belly; and by good words and fair speeches deceive the hearts of the simple. For your obedience is come abroad unto all men. I am glad therefore on your behalf: but yet I would have you wise unto that which is good, and simple concerning evil. And the God of peace shall bruise Satan under your feet shortly. The grace of our Lord Jesus Christ be with you. Amen (Romans 16:17–20).

"Cause divisions" means to stand apart. Some people want others to stand apart. Strife, jealousy, pride, and a desire for power can cause divisions in a church. Divisions can cause harm to the fellowship of the church and a stumbling block to other believers. Paul asked the church members to notice those that cause divisions (17). These divisions were caused by teaching false doctrine.

The greatest damage to a church can be caused by false or misleading teaching that follows the ideas of people rather than the teaching of the Lord Jesus Christ. We should avoid people who cause divisions (17).

Those who cause divisions do not serve Jesus but are only concerned with their base instincts and needs. They fool others by using deceit, lies, and slick talk (18). However, the obedience of the Roman church to the gospel had become well-known in the ancient world. This fact caused Paul to rejoice, but he cautioned them to continue to be wise and discern between good and evil (19).

Divisive people destroy the peace and unity of the church. But God, who is the source of peace, will crush this work of Satan when believers are faithful to the Lord (20). The day is coming when Satan and all who follow him will be cast into the lake of fire (Revelation 20:10). Paul closed with his usual prayer that the grace of the Lord Jesus Christ would be with them (10).

GREETINGS FROM PAUL'S FRIENDS

After closing the message of his letter, Paul let those with him sign it and send their greetings. He mentioned Timothy, his son in the ministry. Timothy had worked with Paul and later received two letters from Paul, included in the New Testament (Romans 16:21-24).

Paul dictated this letter to Tertius, so he sent his personal greeting to him (22). Gaius of Corinth hosted Paul, and the church met in his house. Erastus, treasurer of the city, and Quartus, a brother, also sent their greetings (23). Again, Paul closed this section with his customary prayer that the grace of the Lord Jesus Christ be with you all (24).

BENEDICTION

Now to him that is of power to stablish you according to my gospel, and the preaching of Jesus Christ, according to the revelation of the mystery, which was kept secret since the world began, but now is made manifest, and by the scriptures of the prophets, according to the commandment of the everlasting God, made known to all nations for the obedience of faith: To God only wise, be glory through Jesus Christ for ever. Amen (Romans 16:25–27).

Paul closed his letter with one of the most eloquent and powerful benedictions in Scripture. He declared that God can establish us (25). Establish meant to lay a strong foundation. Paul desired to visit Rome to help them be established (Romans 1:11). Then, he praised God, who can accomplish His will and way for the church. God used the gospel, the preaching of Jesus Christ, to establish the church in Rome. In a nutshell, the gospel is found in John 3:16: "For God so loved the world that He gave His only begotten Son that whosoever believes in Him should not perish but have everlasting life."

God's plan of salvation had been a mystery but was fully revealed when Jesus came. Salvation by grace through faith was being made known to the nations by the command of Jesus: "Go therefore and make disciples of all the nations, baptizing them in the name of the Father and of the Son and of the Holy Spirit, teaching them to observe all things that I have commanded you; and lo, I am with you always, even to the end of the age. Amen" (Matthew 28:19-20 NKJV). All praise is directed to God, the source of all wisdom. Our praise is directed to God forever because of Christ Jesus (27).

CONCLUSION

Jeremiah challenged the people: "Stand in the ways and see, and ask for the old paths, where the good way is, and walk in it; then you will find rest for your souls …" (Jeremiah 6:16 NKJV).

The old path was the way of faith in the Lord that Abraham, Isaac, and Jacob walked. The words "Now faith is the substance of things hoped for, the evidence of things not seen" begins the 11th chapter of Hebrews. That chapter contains a roll-call of many of the faithful people of the Old Testament who had chosen to follow the Lord in the faith path.

Jesus told a parable that is recorded in Matthew 7:13-14 about two different ways a person could choose to travel. One was the broad, easy way, the way of this evil world. The other way was the narrow way, the Jesus way. The broad way leads to eternal death, and the narrow way leads to eternal life. You must make the choice.

Today the woke politicians, woke education, and woke media are promoting an atheistic, socialistic climate cult religion that is the broad way which leads to destruction. Jesus bids you to come follow Him in the narrow way, the faith way, the way of belief in Almighty God that leads to life. Some today want to follow the teachings of a man. We should follow the teachings of Jesus.

Which way will you choose? Joshua challenged the people of his day: "Choose for yourselves this day whom you will serve … . But as for me and my house, we will serve the Lord" (Joshua 24:15 NKJV). Will you take your stand on the side of Joshua? Will you declare to your family, to your neighbors, to the world, "As for me and my house, we will serve the LORD"?

www.ingramcontent.com/pod-product-compliance
Lightning Source LLC
Chambersburg PA
CBHW052106090426
42741CB00009B/1694